COUNTING ON YOUR$ELF

A Woman's Way to Wholistic Wealth

JACKIE HENRION

This book is intended for educational and informational purposes only and does not constitute financial, investment, legal, or tax advice. Readers should consult qualified professionals regarding their individual circumstances.

ISBN 978-1-7331672-5-3

Library of Congress Control Number: 2026906458

Published by Studio Decouvrir
St. George, Utah, United States
www.studiodecouvrir.com

Preparation for publication by Turtlemoon Publishing
www.turtlemoonpublishing.com

Cover and book design by Laura Wahl
www.laurawahldesigner.com

Fonts used: Roboto Light, Filson Pro

Subjects:
Personal finance for women
Mindfulness and financial decision making

A practical framework for wholistic financial decision making and life planning.

DEDICATION

To women of the world

To the women whose contributions made this book possible

To the women who inspire me to dwell in possibility and viriditas:
Manisha, Brook, Gabrielle, Amanda, and Alexandra

CONTENTS

INTRODUCTION

There are many books that promise transformation, but this one begins with a humbler proposition: that counting, yes, basic, third-grade counting, can shift how you see your life. Counting can change the way you make decisions, how you interpret the signals of your own experience, and how you come to recognize yourself not as a fixed statue, but as a woman in motion. A woman growing. A woman quietly renovating her inner architecture without waiting for a building permit.

Let's be honest: counting doesn't sound glamorous. No one has ever said, "I took up counting and my whole life opened like a lotus." Counting's most familiar form is just watching sheep fence-leap to get to sleep. But numbers are sneaky little truth-tellers. Especially the truths we prefer to sidestep with a polite smile.

I learned this firsthand in the most improbable of places: a Rolfing clinic in Seattle. At the time, I'd signed up for a series of sessions mostly out of curiosity; one part scientific interest, one part hope, and one part "Well, I'm here, I'm alive, why not?" Rolfing, as it turns out, is the art of persuading your fascia (a stubborn, opinionated tissue) to let go of its emotional archive. Think deep tissue work, but performed by someone whose elbows have learned to do tango ochos on your individual muscles.

My practitioner, Bevin, had recently completed her certification and carried the earnest enthusiasm of a botanist meeting her first rare fern. Before we began, she outlined the system: "You'll rate each sensation from one to ten," she said sweetly. "A seven is the limit. Anything higher and your body will revolt. We don't want revolt." Unfortunately, I got stuck on the idea that my body might be planning a coup.

Because then came the moment when her elbow discovered a pocket of fascia that had been quietly storing anxiety, disappointment, and possibly the soundtrack of my twenties. I opened my mouth to yelp "Help!" But no, my assignment wasn't to emote. It was to count. And eventually, I learned to do it.

A five meant, "This is unpleasant, but I can pretend to be curious." A seven meant, "Stop now or I will start confessing childhood transgressions." Anything above that meant we'd reached territory better studied by archaeologists than massage therapists. And here's what shocked me: the more accurately I counted, the deeper the work could go. My body listened. It adjusted. By the end of each session, I felt taller, more fluid, and slightly suspicious that gravity was suddenly working in my favor. I even walked up Capitol Hill with a spring. The kind of spring you get only when your fascia has agreed to release its stuckness.

This was my initiation into the scandalous idea that our own data, our actual sensations, feelings, and intuitions, might be worth listening to. Which, of course, most of us were never taught. We're trained to look outward for evaluation: parents, teachers, bosses, partners, GPS apps, or strangers with unsolicited opinions. Without external validation, many women drift, nudged by convenience, crisis, caffeine, and the occasional romantic misadventure, hoping the next phase of life comes with instructions.

Meanwhile, the world around us keeps shifting. The terrain women navigate today looks nothing like the map handed to us. What worked for our mothers doesn't necessarily work for us; what works for us may mystify our daughters. The landscape keeps moving. The old signs blur. A truth emerges slowly: That the only compass worth trusting becomes the one we build from within.

Which brings us back, happily, to counting.

Throughout this book, after most sections, you'll find a question mark with a blank line. That's your cue to record a number from zero to ten: Your personal resonance scale. Zero if it doesn't apply. Ten if it lands with the clarity of a temple bell. Anything in between is a note from your inner barometer. If you feel inclined, add a few words for the future you. You're not tracking universal truths, you're tracing the outline of your own.

This exercise serves three purposes:

- First, it teaches you to treat feelings as information rather than intruders. As *Women's Ways of Knowing* describes, women move from silence to inner authorship over time. We begin on the sidelines and we eventually take the pen. But no one hands us the pen, we need to practice. Counting is practice.
- Second, your numerical trail becomes a map. Instead of flipping back through the book wondering which parts stirred something alive in you, you'll know exactly where your pulse jumped.
- Third, if curiosity nudges you, you can visit countingonyourself.com to see how your responses compare with other readers. Not to compete, but more of a self-discovery to widen your sense of possibility. Every woman's starting point is different. Every woman's scaffolding is different. Seeing the collective pattern doesn't blur your individuality, it sharpens it.

But whether you ever share a number or keep them private, you'll have begun the deeper work: listening inward, discerning what's true for you, and gently, almost secretly, constructing a life that feels like yours.

And here's the intimate part, the part I wish someone had said to me years earlier: Counting isn't about the numbers. It's about finally hearing yourself. It's about refusing to disappear into other people's expectations. It's about waking up a little more each time you say,

"This is what I feel. This is what I know. This is where I am."

It's about returning, again and again. to the one relationship that shapes everything else: The one you have with yourself. And that, my new friend, is where the real transformation begins.

Workbook

This book introduces a way of thinking about wealth that includes both money and the less visible assets that shape a life: energy, attention, health, relationships, learning, and purpose.

The companion workbook is where that thinking becomes practice. You don't need to use the workbook as you read, and you do not need to complete it in order. Some readers like to move back and forth between the two. Others prefer to finish the book first and then work through the exercises over time.

The workbook is designed to be flexible, revisit-able, and personal. It includes practical worksheets, reflection prompts, and ledgers that help you gather information about your own life and notice patterns that are easy to miss when everything stays in your head.

Use it in whatever way supports you best. The goal is not completion. The goal is clarity.

The Counting On Yourself workbook is available in both physical and digital formats. You can learn more, order a printed version, or download individual sections at: www.countingonyourself.com.

CHAPTER 1

THE QUESTION THAT STARTLED ME – AND STARTED ME

1.1

If I were a betting woman, I'd put my money on this event: Every woman will experience at least one unmistakable WTH moment in her life (a gentler, female cousin of the New York–born WTF). It's the moment when you think everything is proceeding more or less according to plan, and reality reaches across the table and flips it over. These moments arrive without warning. No one asks if you're ready. And while the details differ, I would wager you already have one of your own. Here is mine.

It was a summer evening of rare fair weather; the kind Seattle gets only when nature wants to remind us that beauty's not a myth but her most persuasive argument. I arrived home late, still carrying my workday residue. I collapsed into the creaky director's chair on the back deck of the Queen Anne house we had recently restored to its former architectural elegance. The sun was setting behind the Space Needle in an almost theatrical display. Magnolia blossoms, released their perfume into the warm air.

My husband had poured two glasses of red wine. I assumed he was preparing to toast my approaching birthday. Or perhaps to acknowledge our industrious renovation. Instead, in a voice both quiet and resolute, he said, "Jackie, I want a divorce." At first, I waited for the punchline.

After nearly twenty years of shared high points and heartbreaks, most notably the grief of trying and failing to become parents, I believed we had already survived the worst. But then I noticed the slight quiver of his lips. You know, like the tell of a child overwhelmed.

That was when a twisting sensation began at my shoulders and traveled down into my gut, as if the internal scaffolding holding my life upright had quietly begun to loosen.

?_____

1.2

Reality, which only moments before had seemed like a dependable structure, suddenly took on the consistency of days-old pudding. Large grey buildings of certainty drifted in that flow, dissolving at the edges. In the days and months that followed, through disbelief, anger, resignation, and the deep valley of sadness, I found myself returning again and again to the same bewildering questions: Who am I? What do I value? What is my worth?

?______

1.3

To my surprise, those very questions, led by Who am I?, became the thread that guided me back to resilience, and eventually to a steadier form of mental health. Women experience shock in endless variations: abandonment, neglect, divorce, death of a partner, abuse, religious rupture, betrayal, and the long shadows of PTSD. When I attended the Women in Leadership conference in St. George, Utah in 2024, I was struck by the strength of the women organizing the event and the courage of those who shared their stories. And yet, beneath their varied experiences, a similar refrain echoed through them all: Who am I, and what is my value?

?_____

1.4

During the year my divorce unfolded, I developed a way to answer that question. A method that allowed me to define myself rather than be defined by circumstances. This approach helped me:

- Find the real, lasting love of my life,
- Choose a creative path aligned with my actual abilities and inner knowledge,
- Discover a steadier kind of happiness, success, and peace of mind.

Fortunately, my work life had trained me well. As a purchasing executive in manufacturing, I was accustomed to calm analysis in turbulent conditions. I leaned on the financial tools I'd learned in graduate school and the business sense I'd sharpened over twenty years of management. Those tools became stabilizers, while the rest of my life was busy rearranging itself.

?_____

1.5

In hindsight, I might have recognized all this much earlier. After graduating from Bates College, I launched myself from New York City to San Francisco with the confidence of someone who had no earthly idea what she wanted to do. My psychology degree turned out to be completely useless for employment, and yet, ironically, absolutely essential for ultimate happiness. It seems life has a sense of humor that flirts with philosophy.

?_____

1.6

If I had possessed the inventory system described in this book back then, I could have spared myself several years of bewildered wandering. Eventually I learned that counting on myself at the end of each year, actually evaluating my assets, choices, and growth, gave me the information I needed to approach life's upheavals with more ease. Every obstacle, setback, and opportunity became more navigable. Asking "Who am I?" turned out to be the fulcrum that shifted everything; decisively, and for the better.

?_____

1.7

Readers of this book will gain a systematic approach to answering that question for themselves. I believe we've been misled by vision boards, affirmations, desire-setting, and even budgeting. Each of which has its merits, but only when paired with an honest understanding of who we are right now. Without that starting point, we aim toward goals that outpace our current capabilities, setting ourselves up for discouragement. Contemplative traditions across cultures warn that desire, untethered from self-knowledge, is a direct path to suffering. In contrast, knowing oneself is the bedrock of wisdom. A self-inventory and a tracking system are not luxuries; they are the very grammar of progress.

?_____

1.8

This book introduces a unique approach that blends the science of mindfulness with the practical tools of business and money management. My promise is to keep the language simple, engaging, and, most importantly, free of nonsense. Everything I teach here I've actually done. I learned what worked, discarded what didn't, and refined the system through daily practice, yearly cycles, and ultimately teaching others.

?____

1.9

I'm not famous, nor an influencer, both of which seem exhausting activities.. What I do have is an unusual combination of knowledge and skills, just as you will discover about yourself when you complete the inventory in this book. I have a background in the arts, which has carved intuitive pathways through the right, creative side of my brain. But I also possess robust analytical skills, which crank away quite happily in the left side among language, logic, and mathematics. If you wish to explore that story further, you'll find it in "About the Author."

?____

1.10

My aim is to make these concepts accessible. Each chapter shares an idea, a personal illustration, and a place for you to reflect. Letting you test how the idea lands, and whether it invites you to shift something in your own choices.

?____

1.11

Though this information is valuable for everyone, I am speaking directly to women. Too often, we were never taught how to manage ourselves in this way. These tools are empowering, both for personal clarity and for healthier partnerships. While this book may prove useful for men, women face cultural obstacles and struggles that are different. My thirty-year-old granddaughter recently remarked, "I'm so grateful I learned how to assess and manage my assets. So many of my peers, even those with accounting jobs, don't use these tools personally." Knowledge alone is not enough; integration matters.

?_____

1.12

I didn't learn most of this in school, which is precisely why I offer it here in one place. Many women experience anxiety around money and self-value, not because they lack intelligence, but because they lack guidance, support, and feedback. I often hear women say, "My husband is better with numbers," or "My nephew handles that stuff, so I trust him." The difficult truth is that our society has long preferred women to remain dependent. The cultural story says men are the earners and women the spenders. It's a myth so outdated it should be archived in a museum of bad ideas. It's time we evolve.

?_____

1.13

Even if you work with a professional financial advisor, you should understand the principles in this book before choosing one. That way, you can ask informed questions, request meaningful reports, and evaluate whether their guidance aligns with your needs. One of my former students, Kristin, told me, "We just hired a fiduciary. But because of your class, I actually understood everything he said. And I'd already done most of the work he wanted us to do." In other words, knowledge begets confidence, and confidence begets agency.

?_____

1.14

I've reflected on why women have historically relied so heavily on others in matters of power, money, and self-direction. The simplest explanation may be the truest: these skills grant power. And many men behave as though our power threatens theirs. Women are encouraged to be attractive, supportive, compliant, nurturing, and most of all, quiet. But silence, by itself, rarely results in the necessary road-tested wisdom that helps us thrive.

Here's an illustration. After I explained this strategy to Lisa, she shared it with her husband, Rick. Her husband said, "You know, Lisa, not everyone is as analytical as Jackie." Lisa was hurt and confused by his reaction. She felt discouraged and puzzled. I suggested, "Don't take it personally. Men don't realize what they're doing because they can't help but absorb the norms of our culture. Just keep learning about yourself as you nudge them towards a more reasonable frame of reference."

It was interesting that a year later, I had a conversation with Rick. He said, "Lisa is all about assets now. She talks to all her friends about it!" I even detected a hint of pride in his voice.

?_____

1.15

To add power and wisdom to your life, you must cultivate them yourself. That is why this book is called ***Counting On Yourself***. I want to offer every woman, especially the younger ones just beginning their adult lives, tools to help them navigate the cliffs, uncertainties, and turning points that nearly every woman encounters.

?_____

CHAPTER 2

THE DEFINITION OF MIND

2.1

At the center of this mindful money strategy is a definition created by the psychologist Daniel J. Siegel. A definition so deceptively simple and unexpectedly elegant that it has rearranged how I understand nearly everything. Siegel tells a story in his seminars about traveling to meet the Dalai Lama while researching the mind. Since Siegel was a scientist studying consciousness, it seemed reasonable to consult a man whose career, so to speak, is Mindfulness itself. According to Siegel, the Dalai Lama said something along the following lines:

> **"You in science must take the lead now. We in the spiritual field have failed to convince humankind to live in peace with themselves and others."**

Imagine being handed that assignment! Then, years later, after one of Siegel's academic presentations, a monk approached him and said, "Thank you for describing what we do in practical, useful terms." In other words: Thank you for translating the ineffable into something humans can actually use.

?_____

2.2

My undergraduate degree was in psychology, and when I first heard Siegel's definition, I felt the kind of internal click one experiences when hearing a perfect musical chord. Leonard Cohen's "perfect chord," to be precise.

The definition comes in two parts:

First: The mind is a process of regulating energy and information.

Second: That process is emergent, self-organizing, embodied, and relational.

The first part is refreshingly straightforward. The second part requires a bit more unpacking, which I'll do in the next chapter. For now, we begin with the first, because it can immediately illuminate the daily decisions that shape our lives.

?____

2.3

Siegel developed this definition after assembling an interdisciplinary panel of scientists; neuroscientists, psychiatrists, physicists, contemplatives. In this way, he could study the mind with some semblance of rigor. After receiving his doctorate from Harvard and joining the psychology faculty at UCLA, he founded the Mindsight Institute.

He wanted to understand why experienced meditators were so capable of regulating their behavior, cultivating peace of mind, and navigating difficulty with an ease that seemed almost unfair. He wanted to adapt their strategies for use in his therapeutic practice. He coined the term Mindsight to describe this ability, because although it grew from contemplative traditions like yoga and meditation, he believed the principles could be translated into practical, science-based methods. And for our purposes, this matters because those same methods can help us manage both our money and our non-money assets much more skillfully.

?____

2.4

By calling the mind a process, Siegel sidestepped several thousand years of philosophical squabbling. Thinkers since ancient Greece have argued about whether the mind is a physical object (like the brain) or an invisible abstraction (like the soul). Siegel took a more useful path. He said, essentially: Let's not argue about the furniture. Let's study the function.

To explain the mind as a process, he uses the example of learning to drive. We learn what the gas pedal does (energy), how the gauges and signs work (information), and how to coordinate the two so we don't end up in a ditch. Driving is a process, skillful, learnable, imperfect, evolving. Likewise, he suggests that what we do with a car is drive; what we do with ourselves is mind. In other words: the mind is not a thing we possess, it's something we do.

When I first encountered his theories, I actually laughed out loud. It felt as though Siegel had performed an academic magic trick. He essentially told the entire field of psychology, "You all keep debating Freud, Pavlov, behavioral conditioning, id-ego-superego, and long-suffering childhood traumas. Meanwhile, we'll be over here teaching people how to operate their inner vehicles without driving off emotional cliffs." It was an elegant reframing, one that took a snarled philosophical knot and replaced it with a simple gear shift.

?_____

2.5

After sitting with the definition, I realized something else: if we broke down the biggest decisions of our lives the way we break down the components of driving, we could make those decisions with far more skill. We could learn to tune into our own internal dashboard, gauges we all possess but rarely know how to read.

Yes, we have instincts for danger, joy, longing, pain, and love. But these instincts can become unreliable during emotional turbulence. When my first marriage ended, my therapist would ask how I felt about certain events, and I discovered, to my embarrassment, that I had almost no vocabulary for my internal world. I could not name my feelings, nor gauge their intensity. I needed clearer data: my own data. And that is one of the core skills you'll learn when we reach the section called Mind Money.

?_____

2.6

So what exactly does Siegel mean when he talks about the regulation of energy? This is where things get unexpectedly entertaining. Siegel often recounts his frustration when he asks fellow scientists to define energy. They say, "We don't know."Then, when pressed, they reluctantly offer, "Well... it's a potential. A potential to do stuff." (A highly technical description, as you can see.)

But for our purposes, we will focus on three specific forms of "potential":

Emotional energy: the ancient, instinctive biochemical currents we experience from the oldest structures in the brain.

Attentional energy: the focused mental force we generate when we direct our awareness.

Financial energy: the stored symbolic power we call money.

As you move through this book, you will see that learning to regulate these three forms of energy: emotion, attention, and money, often determines whether a life moves toward just surviving, being stuck, detrimental dysfunction, or thriving by learning how to focus and allocate your energy.

?_____

2.7

Information, much like energy, can mean many things depending on whom you ask. For our purposes, we'll define information more simply: data that is useful for survival. Every living system, from a leaf to a lion to a human being, must develop sensory mechanisms to interpret its environment and make skillful choices. That is information.

This is where General Systems Theory (GST) becomes helpful. GST teaches us that although we are constantly bombarded with sensory input, successful systems don't just absorb information, they filter, interpret, and, crucially, adjust based on feedback.

You may have noticed, with mild annoyance, that companies often send customer satisfaction surveys after you buy something. That is their information feedback loop.

In this book, your feedback loop is the Financial Selfie. It is your way of observing, year after year, whether your choices are moving you toward growth, balance, and resilience, or nudging you toward stress, depletion, or stagnation. It is the loop that reveals whether you are thriving.

?_____

2.8

This book will give you new tools for minding. Tools that help you learn from your life experiments and make informed, self-authored choices. You might even think of these tools as measurement devices. Like the way your parents measured your growth by making a yearly mark on the door frame. I sometimes feel a hit of gratitude for the person who invented the measuring cup. Prior to that a "cup" of something might mean a teacup, a beer stein, a ceramic mug or a tin miner's cup. But as society progressed, we learned to standardize the measuring cup at 8 ounces, marked on the side of a glass. In fact, that set of marks might also include milliliters, which helps us use recipes from different cultures.

Once you begin counting on yourself, you'll gather practical information that will inform your choices. You can develop your own recipe for a better life. And if you continue, you'll discover the quiet confidence of someone who can navigate life with skill rather than accident, clarity rather than chaos.

?_____

CHAPTER 3

THE MINDING PROCESS

3.1

The terms Siegel uses to describe the Minding process may feel slightly foreign at first: emergent, self-organizing, embodied, and relational. They sound like they could belong to a graduate seminar or perhaps an unusually philosophical yoga retreat. But don't worry, we'll take them one at a time so you can see how each applies not only to the mind but to your daily decisions, your relationships, and the ways you navigate your own life.

?_____

3.2

Let's begin with emergent. In Siegel's view, when you learn to "mind" yourself, much like learning to drive, your behaviors and choices cannot always be predicted. This idea comes from chaos theory, which delighted mathematicians and deeply annoyed traditional psychologists. You see, psychology has spent more than a century trying to explain and predict human behavior through various models: Freudian, Behavioral, Cognitive, Gestalt, Jungian, Humanist, you name it. Each one tries to map the terrain.

But Siegel's use of "emergent" acknowledges a truth we've always known intuitively: life is in constant motion. Circumstances shift. Opportunities appear and vanish. Your formative conditions are unique, and so are the choices you make. In other words, your success depends less on fitting into a model and more on learning to make decisions that arise from your current conditions, your creativity, your intuition, your real-time awareness. Skillful choices emerge from this intersection.

Even so, we humans have a pesky tendency to prefer the familiar. Psychologist Daniel Kahneman, who later earned a Nobel Prize, demonstrated this convincingly. His research demonstrated that the brain evolved to conserve energy. Unfortunately new learning takes more energy than old habits. So we lean toward what is familiar, even when it no longer serves us. See that word energy? That's why his Nobel Prize was in economics, not psychology. His work provides the the connection between the mind and money.

If this sounds eerily like your relationship to money; fear, hesitation, or the occasional craving, it's not because you're flawed. It simply means your brain is doing what brains are designed to do: defaulting to childhood patterns.

This book offers tools to recognize those patterns, evaluate them, and, when needed, choose differently. You are not condemned to roads that lead nowhere. You can turn the wheel.

?_____

3.3

Now we arrive at self-organizing. Humans have been categorizing experience for millennia: "good," "bad," "right," "wrong," "successful," "unsuccessful." The ancient greek philosopher Aristotle wrote volumes on such ethics long before we had scientific vocabulary for the process. Siegel explains that we internalize those categories in two ways:

Top-down (what we are told to believe), and

Bottom-up (what we learn through our direct experience).

This is why we notice when a parent instructs us to "be a

good person" yet behaves in ways that are hurtful or inconsistent. Our minds register the contradiction. We are always organizing ourselves, sorting, interpreting, reconciling the world inside us with the world outside us.

These early contradictions often lead to what Siegel calls dis-regulated strategies; rigid or chaotic responses. When it comes to money, most of us learned by observation, not instruction. A parent may preach frugality but spend impulsively. Another may stress caution but avoid financial planning altogether. Another may talk about love, but neglect, or worse, use money as a stand-in for love. We internalize these mismatched messages. And then we try, often clumsily, to organize them into some workable adult philosophy. No wonder money feels confusing. We're reconciling the financial equivalent of mismatched furniture inherited from multiple generations.

Siegel points out that the process of reconciling these inner and outer worlds, what he calls integration, is lifelong. But the encouraging part is this: integration improves when we establish a feedback loop. That's where this book comes in. By learning to track your own growth and observe your choices, you create the very conditions that allow for better decisions and greater resilience. A small amount of information, honestly gathered, gently interpreted, can change everything.

?______

3.4

Next comes embodied. This term emerges directly from Siegel's clinical work. He noticed that advanced meditators regulate their emotions through physical awareness: breath, posture, or subtle muscle cues. These practices may sound lofty, but they're surprisingly practical. When we observe the breath, slow it, or deepen it, we shift the energy of the mind. In Vipassana practice, students learn to scan the body with patient curiosity, noticing where tension sits and how it moves.

When I began doing this myself, I discovered that I raised my left eyebrow, like Vincent Price's piercing stare, whenever my mind began to chatter. It was both amusing and informative. If I relaxed the eyebrow, the chatter softened. My anxiety lessened.

Money, for many women, is a source of bodily tension. Learning to notice where you hold that tension is the first step in learning to dissolve it.

?_____

3.5

Finally, interpersonal, or what Siegel most recently calls relational. Nothing in our development happens in isolation. We are shaped by the people, conditions, family dynamics, and cultural systems around us. And in turn, we shape them. This matters enormously when it comes to money and non-money assets. Our energy expands when we manage our relational world wisely, and depletes when we don't.

For example, I know a woman who is a counselor, dedicated entirely to helping others: friends, family, clients. But sometimes at the expense of her own energy and development. She gives generously, until her health falters, her sleep is disrupted, and her relationships disappear under pressure. Recently, however, has she begun practicing contemplative work, self-valuation, and actual rest, slowly bringing her system back into balance.

?_____

3.6

This idea of interpersonal resonated with me because, during my psychology studies in the 1970s, General Systems Theory was gaining momentum across many fields. In simplified terms, it teaches that individuals are continuously shaped by surrounding systems, family, culture, community, and simultaneously shape those systems from within. Growth depends on locating and understanding feedback loops: where attention is placed, where energy flows, where internal and external information meet. The chapter on Mind Money will give you tools to create and track precisely these kinds of loops.

?_____

3.7

It is unfortunate that many women today are still encouraged, sometimes subtly, sometimes loudly, to depend on others rather than develop their own internal authority. We hear phrases like "safety in numbers," and indeed, friendships and chosen communities often create bonds where emotional and sometimes even financial support are shared. Sometimes this works beautifully. And sometimes it doesn't. This may not be the best guidepost for your life.

One of the most complicated interpersonal terrains for women is choosing a life partner. For many of us, that choice becomes a swirling combination of emotion, attraction, timing, and hope. But I learned something powerful during my divorce, something that ultimately changed what I looked for in partnership. I told myself, quite plainly, I want a partner who can articulate his feelings and who has at least as much personal infrastructure, both emotional and financial, as I did, so that we can grow together. It felt both practical and aspirational, the way a good guiding principle should.

During that time, I began taking art classes. For a student show at a local gallery, I noticed a man helping to hang our work. He was undeniably handsome; long, muscled limbs, a trim frame, and a sweet, curly ponytail that gave him the air of a adventurous woodland spirit. But he was wearing worn jeans and an old t-shirt, and I remember thinking, with a mix of curiosity and caution, I don't need to entangle myself with a starving artist. So I mentally filed him under "no-go." At the final class of the term, however, the teacher introduced him as our model for the day. Out of curiosity more than intent, I invited him to lunch.

What followed was one of those fairy-tale lightning-bolt encounters that rearrange the internal landscape. On the walk back to class I found myself thinking, somewhat to my own astonishment, "I would sell my soul for a relationship with this man." Fortunately, it didn't come to that. He felt the same lightning bolt. But a few months in, he hinted that he might have enough money to support us both, should I be willing to stop working. And here is where the years of self-inquiry mattered. I had spent the difficult period after my divorce learning who I was, truly, and I was not about to abandon that clarity for a handsome artist-sailor who happened to live on a boat in Shilshole Bay. So I asked to see the numbers. I laid everything out using the Financial Selfie. And to my surprise, and relief, it made energetic sense. The patterns were stable. The partnership was balanced. We could build a life as a team. He was impressed.

We have used the Financial Selfie ever since to ensure that our shared goals and lifestyle choices remain aligned, as our trust has deepened. In fact, once you begin using this strategy yourself, sharing it with a potential partner becomes a remarkably clear, and surprisingly gentle, test of their commitment to growth.

?_____

3.8

Counting On Yourself is intended to help shift your pattern. By learning to track your personal growth year to year, you no longer rely solely on others' evaluations or cultural expectations. You begin to see yourself clearly. This clarity fosters confidence, strengthens decisions, and aligns your path with your true capabilities. And the earlier we learn this, the stronger we become.

?_____

CHAPTER 4

THE SPREADSHEET CONCEPT

4.1

You need to learn about spreadsheets. Full stop. When I first taught this material to mature students at Utah Tech's Institute of Continued Learning, I was warned that most of them had never used a spreadsheet.

"No problem," I said cheerfully. Naively, as it turned out.

"If you can make a shopping list, you can use this strategy."

I meant it. I wanted to reassure them that spreadsheets were simply a structured way of seeing what most of us already know intuitively. A spreadsheet helps you translate your life, your energy, your habits, your money, into something measurable. Something visible. Something clearer than gut instinct or the well-meaning (and often contradictory) advice of friends and family.

?_____

4.2

But as the semester unfolded, I realized how overly optimistic that statement was. The spreadsheet wasn't just a container for information, it was part of the thinking process itself. Its structure, the rows, columns, formulas, was a kind of quiet logic, a way of organizing the mind. And for many women in my class, that logic was unfamiliar enough to become a barrier. A real one.

Not knowing how to navigate a spreadsheet puts us at a

disadvantage when making major life decisions: choosing a partner, evaluating a job offer, investing money, buying a house, relocating, starting a business, or even deciding whether now is the right time to have a baby. These are decisions that shape the architecture of a life. A spreadsheet, surprisingly, is one of the few tools that lays that architecture bare.

Because here's the truth: learning to use a spreadsheet changes the way you think. It teaches you how to track the regulation of your energy, your money, your choices, your time, your growth, by giving you a clean, consistent feedback loop. It shows you, in a way that intuition alone cannot, what is strengthening you and what is draining you.

That's why the simple tool I call the Financial Selfie is so potent. It answers the question "Who am I?" through numbers—your numbers. And even more powerfully, it shows you who you are becoming.

?_____

4.3

It's unfortunate that we rarely learn to ask this question early in life. I remember vividly the first time I asked it. If you don't yet know how to use a spreadsheet, now is the time to learn. Watch a video. Download Numbers, Excel, or Sheets. Open the app and tap around. You can even use yourself, and this book, as your first experiment.

If you already know spreadsheets? Lucky you. You've drawn a very good card in the game of life. Feel free to skip ahead to the Financial Selfie chapter.

?_____

4.4

In some ways, I was fortunate. I was at a pivotal point in my career. I was a purchasing executive with a psychology degree and an MBA. But even with those tools, I made a mistake I think many of us make: I believed that if I could just "find my purpose," everything else would fall into place. The slogans of the time encouraged this thinking: Lean in. Act as if. Just do it!

But during the long months of negotiation and change, I realized something much quieter and much truer: Before I could find a purpose, I needed to figure out who I actually was in that moment.

?_____

4.5

I sensed early on that my inventory needed numbers; values that meant something. So I began simply, tracking money in the Financial Selfie. But over time, I realized that money alone was far too narrow a lens. It isn't the source of happiness, nor the determinant of meaning. There are other currencies that matter just as much: emotional energy, community, health, creativity, relationships, purpose, learning.

As I immersed myself in mindfulness practices such as Vipassana and yoga, attended mindfulness study groups, read recent neuroscience texts, and wandered through videos on mindfulness and physics. A physical trainer and therapist I know, Marc, even described his own insight as a moment of pure lightness; an epiphany so luminous he felt disappointed when ordinary life returned. For him, physical movement became the way back to that clarity.

For me, it unfolded differently. I realized that for much of my life I had carried a low-level mental buzzing. A background hum suggesting that something was wrong, either with me or with the world around me. Then, after all that focused attention, there came a moment when I stepped over an internal threshold. It felt as if I had literally walked through a doorway into another world, one in which the buzzing stopped. In that quiet, I felt prepared for anything. I didn't need to perform, posture, or cling to rules. Suddenly, improvisation felt natural.

From within that new frame, I began developing categories for tracking non-money values; the ones that truly shape the experience of a life. You'll learn about these when we explore the Mind Money asset class using GEMPICKS. That's why the subtitle of this book is A Woman's Path to Wholistic Wealth.

It's wealth that includes money but moves far beyond it. Wealth that feels whole. Wealth that gives you the resilience to meet the hills and valleys of life with clarity and grace.

?_____

4.6

So here's the bottom line: if you want to get the full benefit of this self-empowering toolkit, you will need to learn how to use a spreadsheet. Numbers (Apple), Excel (Microsoft), or Sheets (Google.) They all do the job. Choose the one that feels least intimidating and begin. This isn't a test of your technical ability. It's an invitation to clarity. Are you ready?

Because using a spreadsheet will fundamentally change the way you "mind" your life. It gives you a kind of quiet superpower, one that, unfortunately, has been withheld from many women for far too long. If we return to the driving metaphor: Not using a spreadsheet is like operating a car without a speedometer or a gas gauge. You can do it, technically, but it's a gamble. You're constantly guessing: Am I going too fast? Will I run out of fuel? What are other drivers doing?

Once you begin tracking your information, it feels as though your life becomes a bit more like a well-calibrated, semi–self-driving car. You're still in control, but the dashboard finally lights up with meaningful data. Your financial decisions become clearer. Options that once felt overwhelming begin to make sense. And the anxiety that often accompanies money begins, mercifully, to loosen its grip.

?_____

4.7

I often think about how useful this would have been when I graduated from high school. So many of the choices I made at eighteen were driven by instinct, emotion, or the prevailing winds of the culture.

Later in this book, I'll share ideas about how these same concepts can help children learn to participate in family life with more responsibility; how early awareness of energy, value, and contribution could change the trajectory of a young person's confidence.

But even if you're encountering this now, as an adult, you're right on time. Or another way to look at it is that it is never too late to learn this.

?_____

4.8

As you work through the book, you have options. You can fill in the information manually using the formats provided, you can build your own spreadsheet using the template as a guide, or you can download a ready-made spreadsheet with the formulas already built in by visiting ***www.CountingOnYourself.com***.Choose whatever method gives you ease and clarity. The goal is not perfection, it's visibility.

?_____

CHAPTER 5

THE FINANCIAL SELFIE™ SHEET 1

5.1

When I teach this material, I often begin with two simple questions. First: "Do you know your weight?" Every woman in the room nods with the familiarity of someone who has stepped on a scale more times than she cares to admit. Then I ask: "Do you know your net worth?" Less than half the hands go up.

This is a problem. Your net worth, the snapshot of your personal financial health, should be as familiar to you as your weight, if not more so. To lighten the mood, I often joked with the class by saying "Do my assets look big in this spreadsheet? The answer should be: "Yes, absolutely! You want big, fat, beautiful assets on your spreadsheet."

It gets a laugh, but the point is serious.

?_____

5.2

When I created my first personal inventory, I began with a full business-style Balance Sheet, assets on the left, liabilities on the right. The traditional document used to calculate Net Worth. If you're already familiar with this format, congratulations: you are ahead of the game.

Many women who have worked in finance, accounting, or run their own business recognize this structure from the GAAP principles, Generally Accepted Accounting Principles, the bedrock of trust underlying every legitimate business in the United States. These principles will also become the foundation for something even more important: your confidence in yourself.

?______

5.3

Over the years, I simplified the format so it could do what I most needed it to do: help me understand myself and communicate clearly, and strategize with my husband. What emerged is the first of four tabs in your Financial Selfie. It's the bird's-eye snapshot. The view a Chief Financial Officer would have when assessing an entire organization. Except this time, ***you*** are the CFO, and the organization is your life.

?_____

Here is an example of what your Sheet 1 will look like, along with some sample numbers:

A	B	C
1	Liquid Assets	$15,000
2	Stuck Assets	$10,000
3	Performing Assets	$30,000
4	Negative Assets	$(50,000)
5	NET WORTH	$5,000
6	Mind Money GEMPICKS	$70,000

This simple table creates a portrait of who you are financially—both in money and (discussed later) in non-money assets.

?_____

5.4

A quick word about spreadsheets themselves: Each row (down the left side) is automatically numbered (1, 2, 3...),

Each column (across the top) is assigned a letter (A, B, C...). So each box (called cells,) the tiny rectangle where information lives, has an address. For example, "Liquid Assets" sits in B1. The negative number "($50,000) sits in C4.

Understanding this simple grid of letters and numbers will eventually give you access to formulas that can (and will) shape your financial future. Once you know how to navigate this structure, you gain the ability to calculate, forecast, and evaluate choices with a clarity that feels almost like magic.

?_____

5.5

Why does this matter? Because Siegel's definition of minding; the regulation of energy and information, comes alive in this tool. Your Financial Selfie will show you, clearly and calmly, how your choices across a year have shaped your growth.

In the example above, the person, (let's say a graduate, with a student loan) has a net worth of $5,000. This is the result of adding $15,000 + $10,000 + $30,000 + (-$50,000) = $5,000. The formula you would enter in cell C5 would look like this: "sum (C1:C4.)"

When you first do your inventory, you may even find that you have a negative Net Worth! While that's not optimum, you should congratulate yourself! You have started your path towards growth! The goal isn't that you start high or low, but that the number grows, steadily, sustainably, honestly, from year to year. It's not a contest. It's a trajectory.

?_____

5.6

Here's an initial clue about that trajectory. There are only two ways to grow: increasing your Assets in rows 1,2, or 3, OR ***decreasing*** your Negative Assets on row 4. Negative Assets are debt. That debt might be loans or credit cards. Debt can either help you or enslave you. Let that thought sink in for a bit. But, when we discuss this asset class in more detail in the next chapter, you will start to better understand how to make more purposeful choices about it.

?_____

5.7

During my first marriage, my husband and I managed money through budgets. We believed we were being responsible, attempting to keep spending within the boundaries of income. The problem was that budgeting felt like trying to predict the future with a crystal ball. Building contingency categories felt wasteful. And the whole "mother may I?" quality of budgeting grated on me. It felt infantilizing.

Then came the divorce. And for the first time, I realized something glaring: I needed to understand my assets. Not just "what I spent each month," or what my yearly salary was, but what I ***owned***. What was growing. What was stagnant. What was draining me. Assets, I discovered, were the true measure of progress.

?_____

5.8

I knew budgets inside and out from twenty years in business. But budgets were not designed to empower individuals, they were designed to control spending within organizations.The real power lies with the CFO, the person who sees the whole picture, evaluates asset growth, and makes strategic decisions accordingly.

That's the role you will step into. That's who the Financial Selfie trains you to become.

?____

5.9

At the bottom of your Financial Selfie, you'll find a category called Mind Money. Because financial worth alone cannot measure a life. Category 5 assets are the non-monetary elements that bring depth, fulfillment, meaning, and joy. These are the aspects of life that rarely show up on a bank statement but always show up in the quality of your days.

We'll explore these in detail in a later Chapter 7 because they are the heart of ***wholistic wealth.***

?____

5.10

And here is the really wonderful part: This entire first sheet is created automatically for you. Every number you see here is generated from the more detailed information you will enter in Sheets 2 and 3. The Financial Selfie does the math for you. Whether you build this spread sheet yourself, or whether you download it from the website countingonyourself.com, It organizes your life into a clear, manageable picture.

It's like having a tiny personal CFO living inside your laptop.

?____

5.11

In the next chapter, we'll walk through your initial inventory step by step. You will do this on Sheet 2 of your spreadsheet. I promise, it is far more fun than any traditional budget you've ever encountered.

It's a new way of getting to know yourself. A kinder way. A smarter way. And a way that will serve you for the rest of your life.

?_____

CHAPTER 6

THE FINANCIAL SELFIE™ SHEET 2

6.1

Your First Real Look in the Financial Mirror

Welcome to Sheet 2 of your Financial Selfie—the part where you enter your details and the numbers start talking back.

On the next page, you will see the following categories

- **Liquid Assets**
- **Performing Assets**
- **Stuck Assets**
- **Negative Assets.**

In the first column, labeled First Inventory, you'll enter your starting numbers. Just take a breath, look it over, and get familiar with the lay of the land.

You'll also see several additional columns you'll fill in at the end of each year. These are not chores, they're your private growth chart. They show you your progress, your decisions, and the story of you – in numbers.

A question women ask me all the time is:"Do I do this for just myself or for my husband and me?" My answer: Start with you.This entire strategy is about learning to ***Count On Yourself,*** financially, emotionally, and energetically.

Financial Selfie Sheet 2
Four Monetary Asset Classes

LIQUID ASSETS

	First Inventory	2025	2026	2027
Cash On Hand				
Cash Stash				
Checking Account				
TOTAL	$ 0	$ 0	$ 0	$ 0

PERFORMING ASSETS

	First Inventory	2025	2026	2027
Savings Account				
401K Investments				
Other Investments				
House				
TOTAL	$ 0	$ 0	$ 0	$ 0

STUCK ASSETS

	First Inventory	2025	2026	2027
Collectibles				
Clothing				
Things/Stuff/Decor/ Other				
Furniture				
Car(s)				
Other Vehicles (Bikes, ATV, Motorcycles, RV)				
TOTAL	$ 0	$ 0	$ 0	$ 0

NEGATIVE ASSETS

	First Inventory	2025	2026	2027
Credit Cards				
Studen Loans				
Car Loans				
Other Loans				
Mortgage Loan				
TOTAL	$ 0	$ 0	$ 0	$ 0

If your assets are shared, just divide the numbers in half unless your situation involves a prenup or special agreement (we'll get to those subtleties later). After you complete your personal inventory, if your marriage is built on trust, openness, and mutual respect, feel free to create a joint report too.

If it's not built on those things, or if your partner resists providing you with values of businesses or accounts, uhm, that's a different kind of inventory you may need to take.

?_____

6.2

Liquid Assets: Your "Grab-and-Go" Money

Let's start with the simplest category: Liquid Assets, which is just a banker's way of saying, "Money you can actually use right now." There are two reasons to bring your attention here: Safety and Opportunity.

Cash On Hand

This part can actually be fun. I love hunting through my purses, pockets, coat linings, glove compartments; tiny treasure hunts. Do you have a coin jar? A "mystery drawer"? Count it up. This simple act of paying attention is the beginning of minding, the mindful awareness of your own energy flow. You're treating money as the movement of energy, which makes the whole thing feel a lot less abstract and a lot more personal.

Cash Stash

This is your "just-in-case" fund. A lockbox, a safe, a cookie jar, your choice. Some financial guidelines suggest keeping 4–6 months of expenses, but don't let rules intimidate you. This is about your sense of safety and stability. The number you place here isn't merely financial, it's psychological. It reflects your relationship with certainty, confidence, and self-trust.

Make sure this part of your Financial Selfie is password protected. Privacy is one of your assets, too.

Checking Account

This is your financial command center. If you don't have one yet, get one. Your checking account receives money, sends money, pays bills, and, with a little setup, does it all automatically. Please, for the love of your future self, do the following:

1. Set up auto deposit for your salary or income flows.
2. Set up auto-pay for your credit cards.
3. Set up alerts that let you know when those autopays happen.

In this way, you don't avoid or ignore your bills, you minimize the emotional energy (and baggage) involved. This is the minimum level of "minding" required to truly take care of yourself. If I were to describe the steps and time it took to receive income, deposit income, write checks, mail checks, and balance accounts at the end of each month, you would laugh. If you are still doing that, have a good laugh to shake things loose, because it's time to step into the 21st century.

Research suggests that the roughly two billion women over the age of eighteen across the globe vary widely in their familiarity with these asset categories and the capabilities they represent. The descriptions that follow are written for women who are new to this way of thinking; clear, accessible, and welcoming to first-timers.

At the same time, younger generations of women are showing a growing ease with managing assets and understanding financial structures. I believe this shift marks a quiet but profound evolution;

one rooted in equality and equity at the most fundamental level. It may not make headlines, but it is deeply consequential."

?_____

6.3

Choosing Your Bank

Not all banks are created equal. Spend ten minutes on bankrate.com, type in the name of your bank or the one you're considering, and check:

Do they charge fees?

Do they offer any interest?

Are they financially sound?

Be cautious with banks offering unusually high interest rates, they're sometimes compensating for higher underlying risk. Risk and reward are dance partners in finance. If you're younger, you may tolerate more risk. If you're older, well, let's say you probably don't want a second career as a cashier at Albertson's in your 80s.

?_____

6.4

A Word on Financial Safety

As I write this, the financial world has a few warning lights blinking. There's a lot of leverage, (investments made with loans) speculation, crypto volatility, and frothy behavior in markets that make old-timers mutter, "This feels a bit like the late 1920s." I'm not saying panic. I am saying: pay attention. Small banks and credit unions can be more vulnerable when the financial seas get rough. Most of the time, the government and large institutions step in to stabilize things, but your role is simple:

Keep your accounts FDIC insured (under $250,000)

Stay aware of financial news (yahoo.com is fine)

Don't assume things will always work the way they always have

Awareness = power. Power = choices. Choices = freedom.

?_____

6.5

Your First Aha! Moment: The Spreadsheet Does the Math For You

Once you enter your numbers in the Inventory column, your spreadsheet will reward you with a little burst of magic: the total calculates automatically. The formula in cell B4 is already set to sum everything you've entered. And that total? It doesn't just sit there looking pretty. It also pops itself over to Sheet 1, cell C1 as if to say: "Look at you. You're becoming a Mindful Money Manager." Yippee indeed. This is the moment it starts to feel real.

?_____

6.6

Performing Assets

Think of this category as the grown-up treasure chest of money management. If you're going to spend any time educating yourself about wealth, this is the place to put your energy. Performing assets are the things that quietly make money while you're busy living your life. They are the financial equivalent of a well-trained dog who happily brings the newspaper without being asked.

In simple terms, these assets create energy—aka income—without you having to clock in anywhere. The basic streams are:

Interest

Dividends

Appreciation

Rental Income

Business Income

Most women, whether they work a full-time job, freelance on their own terms, or come into money in some serendipitous way, eventually need to shift into a mindset where money itself becomes an employee. A reliable, not-stressed, always-shows-up employee.

Robert Kiyosaki's book ***Rich Dad, Poor Dad*** popularized this idea. He teaches that rich people don't simply work for money, they collect performing assets the way some people collect houseplants. He even created a board game called ***Cash Flow.*** We bought it and taught it to our grandkids when they were young, because if kids can master video games, they can certainly learn how to track a balance sheet and buy assets with pretend money. The game walks you through earning, investing, and using debt wisely. His main asset growth strategy is real estate.

But here's the catch: that was then, and this is now. Real estate has changed. Dramatically. Individuals today compete with corporations who buy entire neighborhoods before you've even clicked "save search." And real estate, like all markets, moves in waves. It has moods. It sulks. It overheats. It naps. You must decide whether you have the patience to learn property management, understand whether a building will actually produce income, and determine whether you want to hire someone else to manage it so you don't wake up at 3 a.m. over a broken toilet.

The real goal is to start learning the language of assets and the pulse of economic energy. The underlying shape of *every* investment is a wave. Which means that all other investment rules may or may not apply today. So you would do well to learn about Bollinger Bands and Moving Averages. But even if you hire a professional money manager, you should still expect a year-end report that you can actually read without needing a translator or a stiff drink.

One rule of thumb that has stood the test of centuries: **Buy low, sell high.** And if anyone tells you "Don't try to time the market," don't swallow it whole. Pause. Ask questions. Advice is only useful when you understand the assumptions behind it. These days, algorithms and AI programs are looking for these very trends. Financial clichés are not strategy. Understanding is the key to better choices. in fact, if your advisor reports loses, you have every right to ask for a detailed explanation so you can learn from mistakes and shift. These are critical skills in managing your (money) energy. Professionals know how to recognize market trends, swells, and dips, like a surfer looks for that seventh wave. You can too, if you pay attention over time.

Sounds simple. It's not simple. That's where negotiation enters the chat. Negotiation is the superpower that sits at the intersection of "Yes, I'd like that" and "How much can I save while getting it?"

Chester Karrass, legendary guru of the 1970s, taught a famous workshop called "Effective Negotiating®." I took it multiple times, because my job success depended on it, and life keeps handing you new scenarios: houses, cars, jobs, businesses, even vacations. Negotiation shows up everywhere like the friend who always calls right when you're about to eat dinner. I learned that people in other countries think Americans are either naive or dumb because we are so bad at it. I recommend learning it thoroughly—and teaching your kids, too.

In my class, one student asked a very astute question about Performing Assets. She said, "What about Social Security?" At first I suggested that it should go under Stuck Assets, because you can never get those original contributions back. But then I realized that Social Security, at it's best, is a form of enforced savings. And, in fact, at a certain age it will start to pay back. After this question, I added Social Security to Performing Assets.

To determine the value, you can register at https://www.ssa.gov and it will tell you the current value of your contributions. When you get to your information page, scroll to the bottom, which lists the record of your contributions. Take a screen shot of that page. Or a photo. I'm not saying you can't trust the government, I'm just saying...

Note the total contributions on the bottom of the page. That's the value you should enter on your Financial Selfie Inventory, even if you're not old enough to receive benefits. This book is not intended to provide financial advice. I just want to share that I elected to take Social Security at the earliest possible time. I simply don't know how things will be in the future, both institutionally and in my own life. I personally feel that Net Present Value (NPV) cash flow is worth more to me.

Remember: every woman starts from a different point on the financial map. When you do your inventory, some categories will read as zero. That's fine, delete the row. That's real. And spreadsheets are flexible enough to let you add and delete lines whenever you need to.

Some women in my classes, who have been older adults, find they have a surprising amount of "Stuck Assets" when they do their inventory. In order to track the details, they have even added another spreadsheet tab, to capture the totals for all their detailed assets. Their next challenge is how to shift some of those assets into the Performing class. Other women, later in life, come to the mindful awareness that "they have enough." Their focus then shifts to Mind Money, which we talk about in Chapter 8.

For me? I started with virtually nothing after college, just enough to afford hard-boiled eggs for breakfast, lunch, and dinner when I first moved from NYC to San Francisco. Then came a marriage, jobs, an IRA, two houses and a condo. And then came divorce.

In my second marriage, we combined assets, made business loans (interest), bought and sold ten homes and condos (rental income and appreciation), invested in stocks (dividends), and I even studied day-trading on Wall Street (more appreciation plus adrenaline). My MBA and negotiation training were invaluable. We had wins and losses, ups and downs, but over time our performing assets grew because we stayed flexible, alert, and resilient. And yes, we tracked everything with the Financial Selfie.

Bottom line: If you're young, you have time, lots of it, to build your performing assets year by year. If you're middle-aged or older or in a major life transition, this is the moment to get clear. Your future self will thank you with interest. We'll talk more about this when we get to Stuck Assets, which often hold the keys to freeing up energy for true wealth-building.

?_____

6.7

Stuck Assets

Now this category, this one's fun. Because stuck assets are basically the things we love, but they're also the things silently eating your financial lunch behind your back. "Stuck energy" means the dollars are there, but they're lounging around like teenagers on summer vacation: perfectly capable of working, but currently napping on the couch.

When my first husband asked for a divorce, I was determined to keep our beautifully renovated and furnished house. But a house is not just a house; it's a mortgage, taxes, insurance, maintenance, lawn drama, appliance tantrums. You know the drill. At first, I listed it as a "Fixed Asset." Sounded stable and grown-up. But when I got honest with myself, I realized fixed really meant stuck. I didn't need a four-bedroom museum all to myself.

So I sold it. House, furnishings, everything. And guess what? The appreciation gave me far more liquid energy than I expected. Suddenly I could move that stuck energy into performing energy. I felt freer, lighter, and actually in control. Zillow can help you do this math too. Just log in and look up their estimate for your address. In fact, for future Financial Selfies I now list all real estate in Performing Assets. That way, I look up the current value and register appreciation as part of the growth of that asset.

?_____

George Carlin famously did a comedy routine about "Stuff." It remains one of humanity's great philosophical works. Stuff accumulates. Stuff expands. Stuff begets more stuff. Cars, TVs, furniture, instruments, appliances, sporting goods, hobby graveyards, clothing, equipment, doodads, gizmos, whatchamacallits.

When my father died, my mother and I cleared out their country house. I paid for six truckloads of "Got Junk" to haul everything away. Value? Less than zero. Negative assets at their finest.

When filling out your Financial Selfie, estimate your "stuff." It doesn't have to be perfect. Cars have Blue Book values which you can find on the internet, but everything else can usually be assumed to be worth about ten cents on the dollar, maybe, on a good day, with the wind behind you. Go ahead, ***estimate*** the value. Don't get stuck on that right now.

I have lived in ten houses with my second husband. Here's the funny thing, we buy comfortable, quality furniture. But each time, the most efficient way to liquidate is to have several sales, where you invite friends to browse and make offers. Often, we visit those friends and get such a kick seeing our "stuff" in their house. It feels like home all over again. But we are grateful that we don't get stuck on stuff.

?_____

Collectibles (art, jewelry, coins, antiques) can be exceptions, but even then: By the time you pay for appraisal, listing fees, commission, and the existential cost of waiting for that "perfect buyer," assume you'll net 50% of whatever you optimistically imagine. And remember: it's still stuck energy. It only becomes mobile when you actually sell it and move the proceeds into something that earns.

Here's another thing, if you start a small business, everything you buy for that business should be listed under Stuck Assets. Even if you start making money. Because, until you make more than you spend, those assets are not performing without you. When I started a business as a singer/songwriter, and publisher, I bought instruments, amps, speakers, mixing boards, etc. Even when I got copyrights for my songs, they were all listed as stuck assets. Now, I get enough royalties to literally pay for coffee every couple of weeks, but the assets never performed without me, and certainly not at the Bitter End Cafe. At least the business wasn't AI, which has stuck assets valued in the billions!

When you do your first inventory, don't agonize over exact numbers. We are not building the next NASA launch plan. We're gathering a snapshot so you can see where your life's energy is allocated—and where it might be better deployed.

?_____

6.8

Negative Assets

Negative Assets are not "bad." They're simply – honest. They're the financial equivalent of the laundry basket in the corner; you know it's there, you know it matters, and ignoring it will not make it disappear.

In the Financial Selfie, Negative Assets are the amounts you owe. They show up as numbers in parentheses or in red because, well, they're literally pulling energy out of your system instead of putting energy in. Student loans, credit card debt, mortgages, car loans, it's all part of the picture.

Student loans deserve their own paragraph and possibly their own dramatic monologue. The cost of higher education has risen so sharply that by graduation, the loan payments can take a bite the size of a small shark out of your take-home pay. Because these loans are now taken out directly in a student's own name, they can feel like a kind of modern financial indenture. I still believe education is valuable as knowledge, as social shaping, and as a credential, but as AI expands into nearly every business sector, our culture has reached a pivot point.

Increasingly, learning to navigate AI may be just as important as a traditional degree—maybe more so in certain fields. And you don't necessarily need to pay university-level tuition to learn those skills. Another track is technical skills. Construction, electrical, plumbing, engineering. These may prove more recession-proof, and, with apprenticeship, at lower cost.

When you're first starting out, debt can actually be strategic. Working in a job for a few years builds the credit history you need to qualify for a car loan or a small mortgage. If you buy a home during a depressed market, when prices are low and sellers are motivated, time becomes your ally. When you sell, the appreciation can be substantial, and your strategic use of leverage will have served you well.

Your Financial Selfie is designed to track all this over the years. At the highest level, you only have two ways to grow:

Increase your assets

Decrease your negative assets

Every dollar that moves in either direction increases your Net Worth. If you add to your savings or investment accounts, Net Worth goes up. If you pay off a credit card, Net Worth goes up. If you pay a little extra toward your mortgage principal, Net Worth goes up. Here's an article on bankrate.com that explains how that works. Each time you prepay the principal, you reduce that same amount on your loan principal in Negative Assets. It won't reduce your payments, but it will reduce the time you have to make payments. (In other words financial freedom!) The chart in the article shows how much money you can save in interest.

'?_____

In Chapter 9, when we talk about the "Flow-Grow" report, you'll see something crucial: credit card interest rates are almost always higher than what you earn in a savings account. Translation: it makes more sense to pay off the credit cards before padding your savings. You are essentially plugging a hole in the boat before buying nicer oars.

Negative Assets take on even more significance within a marriage or partnership. Debt can be seductive, and it can be destabilizing. A strong relationship simply cannot flourish if financial secrecy is part of the pattern. Love, no matter how sincere, cannot override math. Women who earn income are particularly vulnerable when a partner carries hidden debt, because the impact shows up not only in money, but in trust, credit scores, safety, and long-term wellbeing.

This is why clarity matters. Talk with your bank. Ask whether there are any credit lines connected to your household that you may not be aware of. If something feels "off, "unexpected purchases, unexplained absences, sudden acquisitions, or patterns like partying or gambling, consider checking with credit bureaus such as Equifax to verify whether any accounts exist under your shared address or financial profile. In rare cases, private loans or undisclosed borrowing can be dangerous to the household's stability.

Please keep your attention on this. For your own consistency and peace of mind, consider setting up automatic payments from your checking account so that your Negative Assets decrease predictably and steadily over time.

Negative Assets are not the enemy, but unchecked, they can become one. When you track them clearly and consistently, they become manageable, movable, and, eventually, erasable.

Again, when you fill in these numbers, the formulas in the cells will automatically calculate your Net Worth on Sheet #1. It's like financial magic, but powered by math instead of wands.

When you complete your Financial Selfie at the end of each year, you'll notice something subtle but powerful happening: You start trusting your own direction. Your decisions begin to feel more adult, more self-evident, more grounded. You're minding your energy. You're organizing your information. You're steering your own ship. Brava. Truly.

Some of my students ask, "Could I do this report every month?"

Technically, yes. If you have four spare hours and a fondness for spreadsheets, you absolutely could. Just remember that this is a snapshot, so all the numbers should be gathered in the same time frame. Early on, you might even discover ways to streamline how you get your account information. (Pro tip: don't wait for paper statements. Log in and look.)

But here's the thing: your Net Worth will bounce around during the year. It's like trying to steer a boat by reacting to every tiny wave. You end up overcorrecting, dizzy, and possibly yelling at the horizon.

After using this method for over 30 years, I've found that doing it once a year, literally sitting down on New Year's Eve day, gives the perfect blend of clarity and calm. I enter the new year lighter, clearer, and more intentional. In fact, setting your direction this way is far more effective than making resolutions (which, let's be honest, tend to evaporate by mid-January).

?_____

6.9

The truth is, money tells only a fraction of the story. Researchers like Sonja Lyubomirsky, Ed Diener, and Daniel Kahneman have shown again and again that income explains only about 10% of a person's happiness, and that beyond basic security, additional wealth barely moves the needle. In other words, even people with impressive balance sheets often carry surprisingly heavy emotional liabilities.

That's why your Net Worth is only the beginning. It gives you clarity, yes, but it doesn't tell you who you are, what energizes you, or how you create meaning. To build real, resilient, wholistic wealth, you need another layer of insight; one that tracks your internal assets with the same respect you give your financial ones. This next asset class is what I call **Mind Money**, and it may turn out to be the most valuable currency you'll ever learn to value and track.

?_____

CHAPTER 7

MIND MONEY™ WAY TO WHOLISTIC WEALTH

7.1

I was about fifteen years into my second marriage — yes, the romantic sailor, model, and emotionally articulate love of my life. And somehow, despite all our growth and good intentions, we found ourselves struggling. Impatient. Attempting to control or correct each other. A creeping desire for distance. Financially, thanks to the Financial Selfie, we were solid. But emotionally? We were horrified to recognize the same patterns that had haunted our previous marriages, even though we were with completely different people.

I had even written a song about this dynamic — the way we project our own unspoken fears and frustrations onto the person we love most. It was called "Maybe That's Me."

You reach out, mumble "morning"

My alarms sound a warning

You're groping for a clue

About what we're going through,

Maybe you need some time alone

Maybe you need to run free

Or maybe — that's me.

Our daily moves, well-worn grooves
Cut in stones of friends and family
But these stones bring us to our knees,
    Maybe you need some other friends
    Maybe you dream what life could be
Or maybe— that's me.
    It's easier to say that you're the one
    The reason for all the things— I've never done—
Night's blanket of rest
Stillborn questions acquiesce
And return to the womb
Of answers inside this room,
    Maybe you need to stretch your wings
    Maybe your walls won't let you see
    Or maybe— just maybe— that's me.

7.2

On the advice of our daughter, who had become a life coach, we went to a group study of mindfulness. For five months, every week, we sat in a four-hour class with about ten other brave souls. We went home with assignments. We watched videos on mindfulness scientists like Daniel Siegel. We read books like Charlotte Kasl's ***If the Buddha Got Stuck***. And every week, we had a follow-up call with the instructor that kept us accountable and moving forward.

For both of us, it became transformative in a way neither of us expected. I felt as if I'd walked through a doorway into a new world, one more intensely color-saturated, mellifluous, perfumed, even softer to the touch. And it felt permanent. Something real had shifted. I sensed a newfound ability to improvise my life, no matter what emotional weather moved in.

I had gained faith in myself to listen deeply and express honestly. And my goals, once tangled in the external, became beautifully simple: happiness and peace of mind.

?____

7.3

This inner transformation felt so valuable, so foundational, that I wanted a way to make it as visible as the monetary assets tracked in the Financial Selfie. And that's when I remembered an odd but powerful asset class that appears in almost every business balance sheet: Goodwill.

Goodwill is a company's way of acknowledging non-monetary value, such as brand recognition, customer familiarity, proprietary processes, management talent, key client relationships, or entire portfolios of software and intellectual property. It's the "secret sauce" that makes a company more valuable than the sum of its parts.

And what do accountants do when they need to assign value to something intangible? One of two things:

- They record the full cost of creating it: marketing, training, programming, research.
- Or they assign value manually (educated guesses) as part of an acquisition, recognizing that the company is worth more

because of its invisible strengths.

It suddenly became obvious: this concept was entirely transferable to the Financial Selfie. Just as businesses track intangible value, we needed a way to track the invisible wealth we build through growth, resilience, insight, community, and practice.Inspired by Daniel Siegel, who loves a good acronym, I scanned everything I had studied in mindfulness, neuroscience, and happiness science and distilled it into a single, memorable constellation of inner value:

GEMPICKS
Your treasure chest of self-investment:

- **G**ratitude
- **E**xperience
- **M**entorship
- **P**hysical
- **I**nsights
- **C**ommunity
- **K**nowledge
- **S**kills

?_____

7.4

But for these treasures to matter, they needed a currency. Here's the basic minimum currency I shared with my students as a symbol of their focus.

Then, I borrowed from business again: Users assign value either by recording the actual cost of the investment, like the full tuition of a college degree, or, at a minimum, $10 in Mind Money each time you make an entry. A gratitude practice? $10. An insight worth acting on? $10. A mentoring conversation? A new skill? A breakthrough in personal clarity? All become part of your real assets.

These are the journal entries that accumulate into a different kind of wealth, one that sustains you, steadies you, and gives you resilience through every chapter of your life.

In the next section, I'll introduce you to Sheet 3 of the Financial Selfie: The Mind Money Journal. Together, we'll explore each category so you can start recognizing these assets more explicitly, and discover the true, often astonishing, value of your life.

?_____

CHAPTER 8

THE MIND MONEY™ JOURNAL

8.1

When I first began studying investing, I dove in headfirst: books, videos, charts, formulas. I devoured everything from price-to-earnings ratios and balance sheets to dividend yields, Bollinger Bands, and MACD waves. I learned about cash flow from rental properties. I read widely about markets, economic cycles, international trade agreements. In short, I spent years acquiring knowledge. But then I came across a quote that stopped me in my tracks.

You may recognize the name Warren Buffett, billionaire CEO of Berkshire Hathaway. Buying into his fund is no small commitment, and his advice is practically scripture in the investing world. In a 2024 Inc. article, his most enduring recommendation was repeated once again:

> **"Generally speaking, investing in yourself is the best thing you can do."**

It was exactly the insight I needed. That single sentence reframed all the research I'd done on stocks, markets, and assets. It clarified the missing dimension in the Financial Selfie and crystallized the idea that became the Mind Money Journal.

I began thinking deeply about how one could actually track an investment in oneself. How do you count the value of personal growth? How do you quantify the lessons that shape you? I pulled from everything that had influenced me: happiness training, yoga, Vipassana meditation, contemplative expression practices from my Naropa MFA, and all the mindfulness literature I'd studied and tested in real life. I realized that the practice of journaling provided the perfect bridge.

Journal entries are commonplace in business accounting to capture intangible assets. The recognized category is called "Goodwill." It's a way that business can capture the value of things like proprietary processes, patents, trademarks, and most recently intellectual property and computer technology. The value of these has becoming increasingly important in our high tech world. An now they can become more important categories to you.

In writing, and in personal growth, journaling is a sacred practice of observation, refinement, and integration. My friend Randy Roark, author of ***The Poet's Apprentice***, is the perfect example. He documented his intellectual and spiritual evolution through his years at Naropa and his career with mindfulness publisher ***Sounds True***. He is, quite literally, the annotator of an age.

The Mind Money Journal became my own way of documenting the non-monetary assets that no bank statement will ever show. When I began writing in it, I felt like an archeologist uncovering layers of unexpected value. Some discoveries were painful; others, deeply surprising. Many of the most profound insights, I realized, were forged in the crucibles of pain and experience. Trauma often drives addictive behavior, as the body attempts to regulate what feels unmanageable. But recognizing the trauma is only half the path. The other half is choosing, deliberately, compassionately, to reallocate your energy, attention, time, and resources toward your own growth.

That realization inspired another song, "Birthplace of

Diamonds." It's about the alchemy of suffering, the way pressure and time can transform our darkest places into brilliance:

She walks on lamb's wool white
Not oozing mud of my moonless night
Her sun rises on a new day
Mine only sets

But I share my tales of darkness
'Cause no way she knows the shame
Of hunger so raw
It makes stealing righteous

Her voice rises with something to say
Mine just slurs to silence

She says, "Birthplace of diamonds
Millions of years
Unearthing the diamonds
Millions of tears
The hurt place of diamonds
Dirt disappears
Leaving a brilliant shine…"

She talks of embracing the slime
As if it were a child
"Cradle it in your arms," she says
"It is the birthplace of diamonds
It is the birthplace of diamonds..."

Not long ago, a woman said to me, "If I could add up all the money I spent on cigarettes and medical care, I probably wouldn't have to worry about my future." And I told her, gently, "Yes – and if you had known to direct that same money toward your own growth, you would have been wealthy indeed." This was before I did my own first Mind Money inventory.

Because when I finally totaled the "intangible" investments I had made in myself: education, therapy, spiritual practices, retreats, trainings, mentorships, creative work: I discovered that my treasure chest of GEMPICKS held over a quarter of a million dollars in Mind Money. It was staggering. And liberating. And clarifying. It showed me, in black-and-white numbers, what I had never been taught to see:

I was already wealthy. Just not in the way I had been taught to count.

And that realization became the doorway into everything that follows.

?_____

8.2

The format of the Mind Money Journal is intentionally simple—simple enough that you can make your own spreadsheet in minutes. Or, if you're using the downloadable spreadsheet form countingonyourself.com, even better. In the next sections, I'll walk you through each of the eight GEMPICKS categories and show how broad and flexible they are. These are the containers for the real treasure of your life: the experiences, insights, and relationships that make you truly wealthy.

If you're setting up your own spreadsheet, here are the basic columns you'll need:

+ Selfie Overview | Selfie Asset Classes | **Mind Money (MM$)** | Flow 2024

Financial Selfie Sheet 3
Mind Money (MM$) Journal for year ______________

DATE	DESCRIPTION [Insert text describing Mind Money in these cells]	G	E	M	P	I	C	K	S

Your First Inventory: A Gentle Wake-Up or a North Star

That first sit-down with your initial inventory might surprise you. If you're at a mature stage of life, the sheer volume of lived experience can be stunning. If you're younger, this inventory works like a compass, pointing your attention toward choices and behaviors that will pay dividends later, exactly like Warren Buffett suggests when he says the best investment you can make is in yourself.

The dates may not seem important at first. They'll likely all be the same, or nearly so, for your initial inventory. But over time, these dates become your personal diary of becoming; your practice ground for emotional regulation and intentional living. Some weeks you'll make multiple entries. Other times you might forget about it for a month. Don't fret. Mind Money is forgiving. When the momentum returns, so will you.

?_____

The Description: Make It Sensory, Make It Yours

Your description can be as long or brief as you want, but give it enough detail to mean something to future you. Think in terms of your five senses: What did it look like? Sound like? Feel like? Was there a taste or a scent? How did you feel emotionally? Who else was involved?

Your spreadsheet box will happily expand to hold whatever you write. And here's a delightful trick: most spreadsheets now have a tiny microphone icon. Tap it. Speak your entry. Watch your words appear like magic. The universe really does love a shortcut.

?_____

The Categories: Your GEMPICKS

The categories are simply guides; flexible lanes that help you see your life in eight radiant dimensions:

- Gratitude
- Experience

- Mentorship
- Physical
- Insights
- Community
- Knowledge
- Skills

We'll walk through each one in detail next. But for now, I'll explain how you'll be putting actual Mind Money dollars into this spreadsheet.

How You Earn Mind Money

You earn Mind Money in two basic ways:

1. Enter the actual total cost.

If you paid $50 for a month of yoga classes, enter $50 under Physical. If college cost $35,000, enter $35,000 under Knowledge. If your nursing training cost $10,000, put that under Skills.

And here's the twist: even if someone else paid, your parents, a scholarship, a generous friend, the value still belongs to you. Mind Money also recognizes the investment others have made in your becoming. As we examine the Flow Growth Report we will talk more about such gifts.

?_____

2. Or enter a minimum of $10 for an experience or insight.

Let's say you write: "I am really appreciating what I'm learning in this book. It's opening a new way of thinking. I feel more hopeful and energized." That's at least $10 under Gratitude.

If you have an "aha" moment that shifts your behavior, give yourself $10 under Insight.

And if you paid $20 for this book? Go put that $20 under Knowledge!

?_____

A Homemaker's Hidden Fortune

If you've been a homemaker, prepare for a revelation. You can count your weeks. The role of homemaker requires skill, knowledge, emotional regulation, and constant on-the-job training. For every year you were a primary caregiver, multiply 52 weeks by $10. That's $520 per year in Mind Money.

Two years checking groceries as a teen? That means you know how to show up, be gracious with customers, work with a team. That's $1,040 under Experience.

And this is just the beginning. Under Knowledge, you'll soon discover a whole list of entries you've already earned. Every one of them is part of your initial inventory and your daily life.

Holy Mackerel! Let the Numbers Tell Your Story

As you go through your first inventory, let yourself stretch. Estimate when you need to. Use your imagination. Add it up! You are not a static creature, you are an unfolding miracle of lived wisdom, humor, heartbreak, learning, and resilience.It's been great fun sharing this with friends; mid-conversation, one of us will suddenly say,

"Oh! That's worth some Mind Money, honey!"

And we dissolve into laughter.

This work is playful on the surface, but profoundly serious underneath.

Why This Works: The Neuroscience of Mind Money

If you do this, even lightly, even experimentally, you're doing something powerful grounded in mindfulness research. You are literally changing your brain.

Every time you focus on meaningful moments, you create new synaptic connections. Your brain rewires as your attention shifts. Old thought-patterns weaken from lack of use; new strengths take shape. You bring experiences into consciousness, articulate them, assign value to them — and the emotional centers of your brain light up in response.

You are cultivating new capabilities in real time.

Your Lifetime Asset

The women I described in the introduction, those who could not see their own worth, would instantly recognize their value in this system. Their Mind Money would be visible, undeniable, cumulative. And here is the best part: Mind Money never disappears. It never depreciates. It never gets swept under a rug or erased by someone else's opinion.

Every category totals automatically at the bottom of the sheet. Then those totals transfer to Sheet One of your Financial Selfie. This is your Mind Money Asset; the invisible capital you've carried your whole life. It is yours. It is real. And it grows as long as you do.

?_____

8.3

GRATITUDE is like the chocolate sauce of mindfulness, pour it on anything, and suddenly life tastes sweeter and more manageable. In my case, it even saved my second marriage. When my husband and I hit a rough patch that felt like it could slide into another separation, our coach gave us one deceptively simple assignment:

"Get a notebook. Open to the first blank page. Write something, anything, that you're grateful for about your partner. Date it. Then leave it. Add entries as often as you can. Come back in a month."

That was it. No instructions on what counted. No rules about length. Just notice something, write it down, walk away. We both rolled our eyes. Surely something this simple couldn't touch the deep, confusing layers we were navigating. But we were conscientious enough to try. So each day, we hunted for something small we could name.

After a few entries, I couldn't help myself. I peeked back. My husband had written that he appreciated my attention to detail. I had written that I admired his devotion to maintaining the house. He appreciated my cooking. I admired his fearlessness in making art. Page after page, the notebook filled with these quiet acts of seeing. Of course he peeked too. But we never talked about it.

By the time we returned to our next session, something subtle had shifted. We were both surprised, and a little amused, to realize that the small complaints had shrunk. The everyday annoyances sounded more like static. Even the big issues felt slightly... less lodged, less sticky.

Our coach explained some of the research on attention and focus, much of which is collected in a **2025 Positive Psychology review**: simply noticing and naming gratitude activates neural pathways that soften reactivity and amplify connection. Gratitude doesn't erase problems, it changes the brain doing the problem-solving. It works in almost every area of life. The insight even inspired a song, "Thanks To You:"

It's so quiet I can hear a memory

A few words you once shared with me

A key to doors I made it through

Thanks to you

It's surprising I heard you through the noise

The typical tumble, girls and boys

A thought more worthwhile than all the toys

A different point of view

Thanks to you, thanks to you

That's a note I should have written long ago

But when you hear this song, you'll know

It's my thanks to you, thanks to you, thanks… to you

You know, I didn't understand it right away

Like a seed not yet ready for the day

But the soil was richer as I grew,

Thanks to you

Thanks to you, thanks to you

That's a note I should have written long ago

But when you hear this song, you'll know

It's my thanks to you, thanks to you, thanks to you...

In the Mind Money Journal, every gratitude entry is valued at $10. It may seem small, but gratitude accumulates fast. And yes, people do try to "game" the system by making things up. Here's the funny part: it ***still*** works. The brain doesn't seem to care whether you're stretching a little to find something positive. The attention itself rewires you.

And of course, if you use actual money to express gratitude, a gift, a dinner, a coffee and donut, then you simply enter the real amount under Gratitude. Either way, you're enriching the one asset class that grows every time you notice what's good: your Mind Money.

?_____

8.4

EXPERIENCE is one of the most lucrative categories in your Mind Money portfolio. It embraces two powerful arenas of growth: Work and Travel. Both shape who we become, yet in the traditional financial world they often receive almost no recognition. We tend to measure work only by the salary attached to it, and travel only by the cost. Mind Money allows you to finally capture the deeper value — the return on the investment of living.

Work: The Hidden Fortune in What You've Already Done

One of my students once hesitated to describe her work history. She'd been an independent salesperson and later a regional supervisor for a cosmetics company, and she spoke of it like it barely "counted." But as she described what she actually did, I nearly fell out of my chair.

Working independently requires a symphony of skills:

- self-motivation
- sales and persuasion

- negotiation
- supply and inventory management
- bookkeeping
- customer service

Essentially, she had been running a mini-company all by herself. She'd done this for years. So we calculated it: $10 per week × years of work. Her total? Over $5,000 in Experience Mind Money. The look on her face was priceless. What she earned was less important than what she learned. For the first time, she saw her work as an asset, not a footnote on a résumé, not a job she happened to do, but a source of capability and power.

In reality, almost all work, paid or unpaid, glamorous or humble, teaches us the very skills we need to function in the world. It shapes judgment, builds communication, develops patience, and strengthens our ability to navigate complexity. Your Mind Money Journal lets you finally count what life has been teaching you all along.

Travel: The Education No Classroom Can Replace

My psychology professor at Bates once asked me how I became such an "unusual young person"(his words,) delivered with that mixture of curiosity and affection professors sometimes have. We talked about many things, but one major contributor was a choice I made before college: I took a gap year.

Part of the year I worked to help my parents with tuition. But then I traveled to France and worked as an au pair. And something profound happened. The historic buildings, the rhythm of daily life, the institutions, and the culture changed me. For example, did you know that Paris has "arrondissements?" These planned sections are like a round spiral out from the center that allowed for continuing growth. Like the Fibonacci circle of growth found so often in nature. It was unlike anything I had ever encountered after growing up in gridded New York City. That trip expanded my understanding of the world and my place in it. Years later, my professor told me that after our conversation, he gave all his children tickets to Europe after they graduated from high school. He had watched them return transformed, even if in different ways.

When I did my first Mind Money inventory, I entered the full cost of that trip, $2,500, under Experience. It remains one of the most valuable investments in my life. There was simply no other place on a traditional balance sheet where such an asset could be honored.

Capturing the Gold in Your Experience

As you fill in the Experience column of your Mind Money Journal, whether for work or travel, take a bit of time to consider. Some people say they want to travel just for the fun, just to get away, read a book, or even bragging rights. But don't waste travel on mere diversion, don't just record the meals, hotels, and meetings. For this journal, include the details that made these experiences meaningful, even if it takes a few minutes of reflection:

- What did you learn?
- What surprised you?
- What shifted in your understanding of the world or of yourself?
- Who did you become because of this?

This isn't just record-keeping; it's recognition, it's reclaiming the narrative of your own growth. And it adds richness, literal dollars, to your Mind Money balance sheet. Your experience is one of your greatest assets. And now, at last, it gets counted.

?_____

8.5

MENTORSHIP is a gem not to be missed. In the Mind Money Journal, you earn a minimum of $10 for every mentoring encounter, whether you are the one receiving guidance or the one offering it. Mentorship flows both ways. And both directions grow you.

I often think of mentoring through the lens of an old Disney companion: Jiminy Cricket. He wasn't flashy, but he was steady. His job was simple yet profound, to help Pinocchio distinguish right from wrong so he could become a real boy. Ideally, parents would play that role, helping us become "real," but life is complicated. Sometimes our mentors arrive unexpectedly, wearing hiking boots instead of halos.

For the purposes of Mind Money, mentorship has a clear definition: A mentor is a person who offers you useful life-navigation insight with no expectation of return. No strings attached. No hidden agenda. Just wisdom offered freely.

That's the key word — wisdom. Advice and wisdom are not synonyms. Advice can be tossed out casually, like confetti. Wisdom takes experience, trust, discernment, and real understanding of the terrain you're walking through. A mentor cares enough to offer guidance that actually helps you become the person you're trying to become.

My First Mentor (Who Arrived Right After the Kerosene Shampoo)

I nearly overlooked my first mentor until I began thinking through the Mind Money inventory. When I was about eleven, my parents sent me to Trail Blazers, a rustic camp in northern New Jersey. Canvas shelters. Cooking our own meals. Laundry. Garden work. The whole bit. And at that age, I was, ahem, a bit of a hellraiser. I got into fights, mouthed off to counselors, and carried around a chip on my shoulder roughly the size of the Appalachian Range.

One day, during a routine head check, a counselor found nits in my hair. I had never heard of nits. Within minutes, I was in a cold shower being scrubbed with something that smelled like a kerosene–soap cocktail designed by the U.S. Navy. My eyes burned, my pride burned, and for the first time that summer, I stopped talking. Afterward, Pat, the counselor assigned to de-nit me, sat beside me on a bench. She didn't lecture. She didn't shame. Instead, she said quietly:

"Look, you have a couple of gifts: intelligence and natural leadership. In life, you'll have a choice about how to use them — toward good or toward trouble. It's up to you. But for the rest of camp, try being more aware of your choices."

I remember sitting there in stunned silence. Something inside me shifted, even though I couldn't have articulated it at age eleven. Years later, as I created my first Mind Money inventory, I realized: That was mentorship. Real mentorship. Pat changed the trajectory of my behavior. That experience wasn't worth just $10. It was worth the full amount my parents paid for that camp. I entered $300 in the Mentorship column and marked Pat as my first true mentor.

Mentorship in Adulthood: Learning to Navigate Power Dynamics

Years later, in my professional life, I encountered another mentor, Colin. He was a retired military man turned cowboy poet (a combination that deserves its own novel). At the male-dominated shipbuilding company where we worked, he helped me decode the unspoken rules, navigate power dynamics, and stay anchored in my integrity. His mentoring style was subtle and brilliant.

He once taught me how to push back on a boss's bad directive without triggering a power struggle. He said, "When a boss tells you to do something you know isn't wise, just say, 'You don't want to do that.'"

The boss inevitably asks, "Why not?" And that's your invitation to guide them back to the wiser path, "which they knew all along." I used this line more times than I can count. It saved projects, relationships, and probably my sanity.

When building my Mind Money Journal, I estimated there were at least 50 such moments with Colin, so that became $500 of Mentorship Mind Money. Each entry represents a moment of skill-building, safety, insight, or growth.

Becoming the Mentor

Of course, mentorship doesn't only come from above. We all mentor others, often without realizing it. We drop wisdom in passing, share navigation clues, listen deeply, or model a way of being that someone else takes to heart. These moments count just as much — and they should. Generosity is a form of wealth.

Every mentoring moment you've offered earns $10 of Mind Money, because you contributed to another person's growth. You helped them see the road more clearly. You walked a few steps with them. And that leads me to my favorite truth about mentorship, one that echoes across spiritual traditions:

We're all just minding with each other along the path.

And in Mind Money, every step along that shared path is worth something.

?_____

8.6

PHYSICAL covers such a wide swath of life that it often becomes the highest-earning category in all of Mind Money. It's also the category that teaches us the most about self-care and self-confidence – often without saying a word. Your body is a very direct communicator. It does not send emails. It sends symptoms.

I think of my grandmother, a tough and vibrant Brooklynite from Brighton Beach. To me, she was the embodiment of pure, uncomplicated love. When my sister and I were small, my parents would drop us at her apartment, which usually meant a full day at the beach; no sunscreen, no snacks in plastic containers, and absolutely no concern for long-term skin health.

Lunch was always a ham-and-cuke sandwich wrapped in wax paper, plus peaches from the Italian stand that were so juicy they ran down our wrists and onto the sand. This was considered hydration.

On rare occasions, all four grandchildren slept sideways on her twin bed, her legs wrapped around us like a human seatbelt. When my parents came to pick us up, I would wail as if my small world were ending. In response, she would announce her guiding philosophy, delivered with total confidence and no footnotes:

"If you've got your health, you've got everything."

That line stuck. In Mind Money terms, she was exactly right. A ballroom dancer to the bitter end, she lived until one month before her 100th birthday. Apparently, cardio plus joy plus Brooklyn stubbornness is a powerful longevity cocktail.

Every time you move your body, exercise, stretching, dancing in the kitchen, or sitting perfectly still pretending you enjoy meditation, you earn $10 of Physical Mind Money. If you pay for a month of classes, record the entire amount under P for Physical. Supplements, health aides, massage, skin care, hair care, and yes, the expensive conditioner you swear is "different"—it all counts.

One of the less cheerful trends of modern life is the rise in obesity and cancer. In response, my husband and I have dramatically altered our lifestyle. We now eat alarming quantities of organic raw vegetables and carefully sourced proteins. We've signed up for detox programs involving colonics — a word I once associated exclusively with plumbing.

We've worked with functional health professionals who speak fluent lab numbers and ask questions that begin with, "When did this start... emotionally?" None of this is cheap. But we include these costs in Physical Mind Money because staying alive, mobile, and mentally present is a non-negotiable asset.

Sometimes physical challenges have roots in psychological history, which means therapists also belong in this category. Competent professional help is always worth it. If your car needed rewiring, you wouldn't just talk nicely to the engine. The nervous system deserves at least that level of respect.

Now here's where this category quietly expands: Physical also includes anything that tends your environment.

- Making your bed
- Putting clutter away
- Cleaning your house (or even just one suspicious corner of it)
- Tending your garden
- Watering a plant without passive-aggressively sighing
- Picking up trash on your walk
- Trimming a tree
- Doing a load of laundry before you are completely out of underwear

Each one earns you $10 of Physical Mind Money because all of them support the space where your actual life happens. Over time, order creates momentum. Momentum creates calm. Calm creates the strange sensation that you might, possibly, be okay.

And finally — a parenting bonus round. This is an excellent way to teach children about self-care. Instead of a traditional allowance, let them earn Physical Mind Money for caring for themselves and their environment, then redeem it for real money. Make it fun. Kids love watching their "wealth" grow far more than adults do.

And let's talk about teenagers. That teenager isn't lazy. He's a systems thinker. It is vastly more energy-efficient to let parents do the chores. Naturally, this leads him to seek a future life partner to maintain the arrangement. Do not train him for that career path. Don't become that partner.

8.7

INSIGHTS are those small, electric moments when something inside your brain quietly clicks into place. Not a parade. Not fireworks. More like a tiny lightning strike that makes you stop mid-sip and think, Wait, that changes things. They can come from a movie, a book, a conversation, or a single sentence that sneaks up on you when you weren't even paying full attention.

I once had a student with a PhD suddenly blurt out in class, "That's exactly what I realized about self-awareness years ago! This just reminded me!" Her eyes went wide. Her shoulders lifted. You could practically hear the internal filing cabinets being reorganized. That moment, brief, bodily, unmistakable, is worth at least $10 of Insight Mind Money. Possibly more, since it saved her from re-learning the same thing the hard way.

But the biggest Insight of my adult life arrived, as many of mine do, at Naropa, an institution that seems custom-built for sentences that knock your inner furniture around.

My professor, Gabrielle Civil, assigned an essay by Gloria Anzaldúa with the unforgettable title "Let us shift...the path of conocimiento...inner works...public acts." I already knew Anzaldúa's earlier book, ***This Bridge Called My Back,*** a groundbreaking collection of essays from marginalized voices. This later piece appeared in *This Bridge We Call Home*, and as I read it, I realized I wasn't just reading an essay, I was watching a woman think her way across twenty-one years of growth.

What stopped me cold was her exploration of women she called Nepantleras — a word adapted from the Coatlicue term for "the space in between." These women, she wrote, were:

> **"boundary-crossers, thresholders, initiators of rites of passage — activistas who listen deeply, rise to their own visions, and then actually do something about them, haciendo mundo nuevo — making a new world."**

I remember thinking, Well, that sounds...uncomfortably familiar. The resonance was immediate and unsettling in the best way. I'd spent my whole life feeling oddly "in-between:" Jewish and Catholic ancestry, a grab-bag of Polish, French, German, and Irish roots and the ever-present woman/man dance of trying to claim authority in a world that isn't always thrilled when women do.

Once I saw it, I couldn't unsee it. I began noticing how many formidable women thinkers, writers, and philosophers had been politely edged out of the canon. Suddenly, my earlier instincts made sense, like why I'd deliberately programmed more women songwriters and poets on my radio show. I wasn't being difficult. I was being Nepantlera-like.

That insight changed my aim. I stopped scattering my energy and began focusing it; toward women's culture, women's wisdom, women's ways of making meaning and moving ideas into the world. This book is a direct descendant of that moment.

And yes, I logged a very healthy deposit of Insight Mind Money for it. Because it didn't just shift how I thought, it changed how I chose. Any time you have an "Aha!" Write it down. That wasn't a passing thought. Your brain just paid you a dividend.

8.8

COMMUNITY is a type of Mind Money we usually learn early; how to get along, how to support one another, and how to be the person who brings the good snacks to family gatherings. When a relative has a health crisis and we're able to show up, every travel expense, meal, or logistical cost can be posted under C for Community. (Yes, even the emergency latte you bought while trying to find the right hospital corridor.)

Donations also qualify. At the end of the year, I total what I give to things like Vipassana Centers, our local arts organization;, and Wikipedia, the unofficial global village elder. I also support writers whose work enriches the cultural bloodstream, like Heather Cox Richardson's Letters From An American or Maria Popova's philosophical jewel The Marginalian. And of course, local community radio stations like KRFY 88.5 that hold up the arts with duct tape, passion, and caffeine. Even when contributions aren't tax-deductible, they carry full Mind Money value.

Friendship: Your Chosen Community

Friendships deserve a prominent place in Community Mind Money. They are the chosen family members who show up with soup when you're sick, tell you the truth when you're delusional, and celebrate your successes like they won the award too. Time spent nurturing friendships, coffee dates, walks, phone calls, planning trips, or simply checking in, counts as Community because it strengthens the emotional infrastructure that supports your life.

Each week I join a Zoom we call "Wild Women Writers." A group of women who originally met in Sandpoint over twenty years ago. At the beginning of the two hour session, we check in with each other, share our ups and downs and our sense of ourselves in the world. Thenwe get to the business of timed writings and readings. This weekly effort has become meaningful to us in a way that's incalculable. Except, that I can log $10 in Community Mind Money for each and every session. As a result, the Mind Money value is over $10,000! Another group of women writers I was a member of had a similar history and we published a book of our collected writings called ***Sandpointed***. All the expenses and time involved in that publication were also captured in Community Mind Money. Consider for a moment how meaningful that asset is, and that there is no other way to capture it's value, except internally.

If you invest money into these connections (hosting a potluck, buying a birthday lunch, planning a girls' retreat, sending a small gift), record it. Sometimes when I read an article thats might be helpful or related to a friend's interests, I send it along. That's worth $10 in Mind Money, Honey! Friendships are wealth, and unlike certain relatives, you did choose them.

Professional Connections: Your Career Community

Then there's the community that supports your professional or business growth. These are colleagues, networking groups, mastermind circles, professional associations, or even that one brilliant coworker who knows how to fix the printer when IT "can't get there until Tuesday."

Time spent attending conferences, meeting collaborators, joining professional groups, or nurturing career-related connections should be logged under Community. So should any financial investments, workshops, networking events, memberships, or business lunches that aren't just "lunch" but strategic development. (You know the difference. One involves fries; the other involves LinkedIn.) These connections are not just social, they expand opportunity, confidence, visibility, and the range of what you believe you're capable of. That's pure Mind Money.

Your Most Important Community: The Partnership

And now, one of the best-kept secrets of this category: Your most important community is your life partner. Whatever the flavor, or whatever form the relationship takes, romantic, long-term, evolving, or in the "We're working on communication" chapter, investing here produces some of the highest returns in peace, joy, integrity, and stability. It simply makes life richer to share a sunset, a moonrise, and the universe of stars.

A partner also becomes your clearest mirror. No matter how enchanted the beginning, eventually your patterns, your stuck places, and your handcrafted childhood coping strategies emerge. Partners gently (or occasionally bluntly) point out the spots where we are hiding, denying, or relying on outdated scripts. Many people leave relationships only to discover the same patterns waiting in the next one. Growth opportunities travel with you. Any therapy, coaching, retreats, books, or classes that help you grow as an individual or as a couple belong in this category. They are always worth the investment. There is something fundamental about sharing a life that deserves your attention.

Another pattern that will appear when you use Mind Money as a basis to discuss the future, is the pitfalls of energy imbalance in a relationship. For example, if you are being asked to "put someone through school," or "care for the relatives," or redeem the partner from dysfunctional behaviors, this is an allocation that may not be in your best interest. It's better to have a more balanced way to prioritize energy for your own growth.

A Dating Idea That Still Makes Me Smile

In an early draft of this book, I had a playful marketing idea: Instead of "Show me the money," couples on dates could say: "Show me your Mind Money." Imagine dating apps integrating it: Mindfully Yours™ — match on assets that actually grow. Or perhaps, a simple dollar total for last year's GEMPICKS, that would provide for a far more interesting way to get to know someone.

Instead of profiles featuring people with fish, you'd see listings of Community Credits, Skill Sets, Insight Points, and Physical Investments. You'd instantly know whether someone values self-growth and connection. And in that case? They're already demonstrating the most attractive trait of all: They invest in themselves, and in the people around them.

8.9

KNOWLEDGE captures the value of all educational activities, big or small. It might be paying for a class, attending a workshop, taking an online course, or participating in free offerings like the University of Pennsylvania's "Modern American Poetry" (aka MODPO) with Al Filreis. Every class session you attend earns you $10 of Knowledge Mind Money.

This category shocked me during my first Mind Money inventory. Throughout my life, I've earned several degrees—including an MFA in Creative Writing at Naropa University at age 65. When I added it all up, Knowledge alone represented more than $150,000 of Mind Money. Education isn't just an experience, it's an asset that should be much more than a certificate on a wall.

Relational & Legal Clarity

Here's one example of Mind Money Knowledge that's worth both your consideration and your tracking. It is applicable to any type of relationship, even if it's not a legal marriage. Because in some states, even living together creates a quasi-legal relationship.

When my second husband and I were considering marriage, he raised the idea of a prenuptial agreement. He had been married twice before and wanted to protect assets intended for his family. At that point in my life, I also had assets coming into the relationship. This wasn't a case of imbalance. It was a case of two adults with histories, responsibilities, and property deciding how to move forward together.

Unfortunately, prenuptial agreements have acquired a reputation for being unromantic or adversarial, especially when one partner has significantly more assets than the other. But in our case, the agreement functioned less as a shield and more as a shared understanding. After more than a decade of building a life and new assets together, we eventually cancelled the prenup and replaced it with a trust. That trust also required legal advice and thoughtful preparation, and it established roles and responsibilities that we continue to take seriously.

Every state has its own laws governing how assets are apportioned in the event of divorce, so I won't attempt to summarize them here. What matters more is this: as a woman, you deserve independent, expert advice — whether you are initiating a prenuptial agreement or being asked to participate in one.

An experienced attorney can explain your rights and obligations, help you understand what is customary or negotiable, and flag any provisions that may be out of balance. This is possible when one party brings significantly larger assets to the relationship. Don't just sign your life away. Explore options with the lawyer about assets created or acquired during marriage, your support contributions during marriage, and keep yearly plans consistent with those understandings. This kind of knowledge lies at the heart of power. Your personal power. And that clarity matters. And here's where Mind Money comes in: any money you spend acquiring that understanding is not a loss — it is an asset. Log it accordingly.

Legal knowledge is not just a piece of paper filed away in a drawer. It is a form of self-trust made explicit. It reduces anxiety, sharpens communication, and shifts the experience from something that happens to you into something you consciously choose.

Inheritance Knowledge

Here is another related type of Knowledge Mind Money. Anticipated inheritances are not assets; they are possibilities. Planning your life around money you do not yet own introduces distortion into both your finances and your psychology. What *is* worth counting is the clarity you have, or should have. about how such assets are structured. That clarity, that you can acquire, belongs in Mind Money, not Net Worth.

For example women, or any children of high net worth families, are often socialized to:

- wait
- hope
- accommodate family expectations
- absorb emotional complexity around inheritance
- Instead, what is powerful, and stabilizing, is a stance that says: "I will build a life that works whether this arrives or not."
- What *can* go into Mind Money:
- Understanding estate structures (trusts, wills, beneficiaries)
- Knowing what is discretionary vs. guaranteed
- Knowing timelines, tax implications, and contingencies
- Knowing what is explicitly promised—and what is not
- That knowledge has real value, even if the money never arrives.

The bottom line is that Knowledge, once acquired, does not disappear. It compounds.

?_____

8.10

SKILLS are a special subset of Knowledge, so valuable they deserve their own asset class. These are life capabilities you have mastered well enough to teach someone else. Skills can come from formal training such as:

- Nursing
- Accounting
- Construction
- Plumbing
- Car repair
- Coaching or personal training
- Negotiation

But skills also come from life itself, especially for homemakers and mothers. Childcare is a skill. house-cleaning is a skill. Sewing, quilting, gardening, budgeting, organizing, every one of these has value.

My first job was babysitting, which I got because I had already learned childcare at home helping with younger siblings. Changing a diaper without mayhem is a thoroughly under-rated skill! As is calming a crying baby. When I read through Dan Siegel's books on parenting, such as "Whole-Brain Child," "No-Drama Discipline" and "The Power of Showing Up," I was deeply moved by some of the strategies that parents could use to make a real difference in family dynamics. I often think that it should be mandatory training for parents. In fact, more and more I see that hospitals offer such training to new parents, along with birthing classes. You can record actual money earned, book costs, training costs, or simply tally the number of weeks you've used a skill, times $10.

Cooking, for example, is becoming a lost art. If you can make soft-boiled eggs, salads, steak, fish, or coleslaw without a recipe, each dish is worth $10 of Skill Mind Money.

More modern skills count too:

- Coding
- Programming
- Digital design
- Video editing
- Playing music
- Songwriting, Production, Publishing
- Music theory
- Any Boy Scout or Girl Scout badge
- Any art form

If you have the ability and can pass it on, it belongs in Skills. And it belongs in your asset column.

?_____

8.11

The Big Picture

The first time I completed my Mind Money inventory, I was stunned: I had accumulated over $250,000 of intangible wealth. And at the end of each year since, I add another $20,000–$50,000 in Mind Money, quietly, steadily, joyfully building an asset class that reflects the richness of my lived experience. This is the power of counting on yourself. You've already built more wealth than you ever realized. Now you get to see it, clearly, proudly, and in writing.

Another interesting thing about using a spreadsheet is that you can sort and analyze the different categories. You can actually observe which areas are more natural for you, and which areas you might want to expand into.

Just like Siegel's original definition of ***minding***, now that you will have more ***information,*** you want to allocate and regulate your ***energy*** to categories that most support your growth.

?_____

CHAPTER 9

FLOW-GROW™ LIKE A CFO

9.1

When I was taking my Master of Business classes, I learned that every corporation, no matter how glamorous, messy, brilliant, or barely-holding-it-together, files the same annual report. It comes in a tidy three-part package: Balance Sheet, Profit & Loss, and Cash Flow.

It was the third one, Cash Flow, that stole my heart. Not because I'm a financial romantic (though I'll admit I find a well-organized spreadsheet oddly soothing), but because the Cash Flow statement tells the real story. It reveals how energy, disguised as money, moves in, through, and out of your life.

Think of it as the energetic weather report of a corporation. Sunny with new customers? Storm clouds of debt on the horizon? A mysterious breeze carrying opportunity from the West? Cash Flow captures all of that.

And here's the fun part: Once you understand this, you become the magician in your own life. I mean that literally. Remember The Sorcerer's Apprentice in Disney's Fantasia? The part where Mickey Mouse tries to command the brooms, and suddenly the buckets are marching all on their own, multiplying like tribbles? That short film has proven a useful metaphor at several pivotal moments in life. It is a perfect parable of unskilled energy vs. skilled energy. You don't need a magic wand, you need knowledge that comes from information and focus. Using this report is how you promote yourself from Mindful Money Manager (MMM) to the more strategic Contemplative Financial Officer (CFO.)

The Flow-Grow™ report is your contemplative version of Cash Flow.

You prepare it once a year, and it gives you a factual portrait, not a fantasy; not a budget, not a wishful list of "new year, new me" resolutions, of how you truly allocated your energy. Budgets, on the other hand are built on conjecture and control. Flow-Grow™ is built on clarity. Budgets hope. Flow-Grow™ reveals. Budgets say, "This year I'll spend less on X." Flow-Grow™ says, "Here's who you already are."

And there's something wonderfully liberating about that. When you see yourself clearly, you naturally grow into yourself. No self-punishment. No restriction cycles. No budgeting apps that guilt-trip you with notifications like, "Have you been to a coffee shop, again?" As every contemplative practice teaches: observe things as they are. Not as you fear they are, or wish they were, but simply, and powerfully, as they truly are.

The CFO Mindset: Focus on the Big Flows

Another strategy that will save your sanity: A Contemplative Financial Officer (CFO) focuses on the big flows, not the tiny leaks. This is the famous 80/20 rule: 80% of your energy can be understood by looking at about 20% of your categories. Translation: You don't need to break your latte habit. You don't need to count receipts like a Victorian bookkeeper squinting at candlelight. Your power lies in seeing the rivers, not the teaspoons.

About That Teenager Who Smoked OP's...

When I was a teenager, I had a somewhat charming, somewhat irritating habit of bumming cigarettes a couple of times a week. If someone asked what brand I smoked, I'd say, "OP's."They'd blink.

I'd elaborate: "Other People's." Delivered with exactly the amount of smugness you'd expect from a teenager who thinks she's discovered the loophole of the universe. I even justified it: "I'm not mooching, I'm connecting. It's social."

Now we need to talk about something that quietly (and sometimes loudly) affects your Flow-Grow: OPM, Other People's Money. And here's the thing, many adults carry a more sophisticated version of OPM into their grown lives. Maybe it starts as a temporary move home after a breakup or crisis. Maybe relatives offer help that becomes a long-term arrangement. There's no need to label this as good or bad. Sometimes it's loving, necessary, even life-saving. But sometimes, it points to deeper patterns that affect independence, identity, and the ability to steer your own life with confidence. Remember: This book is about building the car you drive through life. It's about improving your ability to handle energy, information, decisions, and emotional strength.

Your Flow-Grow™ Report is your CFO dashboard. It shows you clearly whether you are using your own fuel or borrowed fuel, and whether it's time to upgrade your engine, strengthen your structure, or gracefully shift into a new phase of growth. It is not moral. It is not judgmental. It simply holds up a mirror and says, "Here's the truth. What would you like to do with it?"

Students often ask, "Should I complete this report for myself alone, or for myself and my life partner?" My answer is the same as the calculation of assets: start with yourself, especially while you are learning the process. Think of the Flow-Grow Report as a practice run. This is an exercise in understanding your own capabilities, responsibilities, and choices. Beginning on your own isn't about separation or secrecy; it's about clarity. Learning any new framework is easier when you focus on a single perspective first; your own.

In some situations, this may feel awkward or even illogical. If your partner is the sole wage earner and you do not have outside income, use one-half of the household income as your income flow, and one-half of shared expenses such as the mortgage, insurance, and taxes. This isn't a legal statement or a value judgment, it's simply a learning model.

You may also feel uncomfortable gathering this information if you've never worked directly with these numbers before. That discomfort is part of the learning. It signals that you are stepping into new territory, and that step is worth taking.

Creating this report is an invitation to step into your life in a wholistic way: to see how energy, money, responsibility, and choice move through your world. Many students find that this clarity improves family decision-making by bringing unspoken assumptions into view. Others discover that it offers quiet preparedness. Useful in the event of illness, disability, or any moment when one partner must temporarily carry more of the load.

After completing the report, you may find new reasons to appreciate your marriage or partnership. You may also begin to rethink long-held assumptions about your role in your own life. Both outcomes are valuable.

This marks the beginning of a more informed relationship with yourself. Knowledge comes first. Flow and growth follow. Once you are comfortable with the process, you may choose to expand the report to include your family. When shared at the right time, it can become a powerful starting point for trust, communication, and thoughtful negotiation—cornerstones of relationships built to last.

?_____

FLOW-GROW		Year________	
SOURCES:	$	USES:	$
Income - Job		Housing	
Income - Business		Food	
Interest		Transportation (Car)	
Dividend		Insurance	
Rental Income		Taxes	
Social Security		Travel	
Life Insurance		Recreation	
Divorce Payments		Medical	
Credit		Loan Payments	
Capital Gains		Investment	
Misc		Savings	
Gift - Parent(s)		Credit Card Interest	
Gift - Friends		Gifts/Grants/Donations	
		Misc	
		Growth	
		Creativity	
TOTAL	$ 0	$ 0	$ 0

9.2

The Report Itself

This report corresponds to Sheet 4 in your Financial Selfie. The format is refreshingly simple.

You'll see categories for sources of money (energy coming in) and uses of money (energy going out). You can download the template from countingonyourself.com or sketch your own, but the essential thing is this: Customize everything. Your life, your flows, your values, your categories.

This report is prepared once at the end of the year. Younger women often fill it out more easily because many already use apps that track income and spending. But as far as I know, there is no app that captures the full wholistic picture like Flow-Grow™ does.

These entries are totals for the entire year. A complete panoramic view. In the next sections, we'll walk through each category with clarity, warmth, and a bit of CFO-level magic.

?_____

9.3

Sources (of energy) from Job or Business

If you look at jobs from 1950 to today, it's like watching a nature documentary where one species gradually evolves into something completely different.

In the 1950s, most countries were still catching their breath after WWII. People worked a job, singular. They wore hats. They brought lunch pails. Many had pension plans that now seem as mythical as unicorns. Unions were strong enough to say things like, "No, actually, Bob can't weld twelve hours straight without blinking." Corporations grew, production and marketing became sciences, and for a brief shining mid-century moment, the system seemed relatively predictable.

Fast-forward to now, and the word job has shape-shifted into something that would confuse your 1950s grandmother. Between computers, the internet, COVID, and now AI, income has become fluid. Wiggly. A "choose-your-own-adventure" situation.

People today often have three freelance gigs, a side hustle, a weekend project; a pop-up shop, and a YouTube channel. Health insurance? Not guaranteed. Work rules? Optional. Predictability? Hilarious.

This matters because your spreadsheet may not have a single neat row labeled "Job." You may need:

Income – Project A

Income – Side Gig B

Income – Coaching, which pays well some months and vanishes like mist in others

Income – Business, which may be reliable or may be

interpretive dance

Whatever the mix, the Flow-Grow™ Report requires one thing: Record the actual income that actually landed in your actual account. Not the invoices you meant to send. Not the vague estimates floating in your mind. Not the amount your friend said her cousin makes doing the same thing.

If you aren't on direct deposit, fix that. Life is too short for paper checks that get lost under grocery store receipts. You can use your workplace's year-end statement, but it often arrives late. Better: pull the numbers directly from your bank deposits. Clean. Real. Undeniable.

Many women in my classes are retired or semi-retired, working as consultants when the muse, or the phone, calls. Whether you have an LLC or you're simply a wise woman with a laptop, collect your yearly total. If something doesn't apply to you? Delete the row without guilt. This is your spreadsheet, not a standardized test.

?_____

9.4

Interest

Interest income is the tame, well-behaved cousin of the financial family. It comes from things like savings accounts, CDs, and bonds – performing assets that sit quietly in the corner, making money without drama. But interest rates move according to the mood of the Federal Reserve, which sometimes behaves like a parent who changes the household rules based on vibes alone.

As a result, interest rates behave like tides, not switches. When we mistake a temporary low for a permanent condition, we build fragile expectations. When we understand cycles, we make steadier choices. Here, for example is a chart that shows interest rate trends since 1980:

Still, this category counts as a predictable, stable energy flow, and it's worth watching. Banks will never call you and say, "We've decided to pay you more. Just because." You will have to ask, compare, and occasionally move your money to greener pastures. Interest income is usually taxed as ordinary income, something to keep in mind when tallying your totals.

?____

9.5

Dividends

Dividends are another form of Performing Asset income, mostly from stocks. When companies are healthy and profitable, they share the love. When they're not, well, you'll notice. Dividend "yields" are worth understanding. (Yes, you can Google this. Yes, you'll feel smart afterward.) Some bonds also pay dividends, but the tax rules vary.

This is one of those areas where a fiduciary advisor can earn their keep, or where you can educate yourself if you prefer the DIY route.

?____

9.6

Rental Income

Rental income has been one of my greatest teachers, and one of my most reliable friends. It took decades of learning, negotiating, repairing, repainting, refinancing, and refreshing Zillow every time I travel anywhere. (Yes, our household joke is that I can't cross a state line without checking local property prices. Some people buy snow globes; I analyze housing markets.)

Real estate can produce marvelous tax advantages and income streams, if you negotiate well, study the trends, and keep your eyes open for those gems half-buried in economic soil. But rental income is never truly passive. It's a relationship. A long one.

?____

9.7

Social Security

Many of my students are already, how shall we put this?, dancing with Social Security. This venerable institution is basically America's version of a forced piggy bank, created after the Great Depression when the country collectively realized, "Oh dear, none of us saved anything." Roosevelt, in his infinite New Deal wisdom, decided that maybe, just maybe, the government should at least make sure people didn't starve in their later years. Fair enough.

What happened to those savings after 1935?

Well, that's the part I think Netflix should dramatize. Picture it: "SOCIAL SECURITY: The Fund, The Myth, The Spreadsheet." There'd be suspense, plot twists, congressional hearings, actuarial tables that look suspiciously like psychological thriller. I'd watch it.

And now? We face the uncomfortable truth that the system may someday lose its ability to fulfill all promises. Younger people are already side-eyeing their paychecks, muttering, "Wait, I'm contributing to... what, exactly?" It's not hard to empathize.

But for you, if you have ever had a job that deducted Social Security tax, your first empowering step is to sign up for an account at ssa.gov/myaccount. Once you enter your information and scroll to the bottom (past several reminders about how old you are, thank you, federal government), you will see your entire contribution history. If you've kept good records, you can verify the total. If you're like me, and early record-keeping was not your love language, you will simply nod graciously and move on.

Your Social Security benefit belongs in Performing Assets, because it is income that is already working for you. But, when to take your benefits is a wonderfully personal decision. Some people wait to maximize the payout. Others, like yours truly, prefer cash flow now, because:

life is short,
government forecasts are... let's call them "foggy,"
and money in hand today buys more certainty than a theoretical future bump.

This is not meant to be financial advice—this is life experience advice, which is sometimes even better. Record your yearly benefit on the Flow–Grow sheet, and keep an eye on whether this source remains stable over time. If it changes, you'll adjust. You always do.

?_____

9.8

Life Insurance / Inheritance

This category tends to appear more often for women in mid-to-later life. These are payouts that arrive when a spouse, parent, or loved one passes. It is income wrapped in grief — which is why we handle it with care, respect, and a softer tone than most line items. If you are already receiving this kind of flow, enter the annual amount in your report.

A reminder: this is a cash flow report, not a spending wish list. If you receive a lump sum inheritance, record it initially as incoming cash. But then, this is the important pivot, you want to re-see it as a Performing Asset.

Why? Because money that arrives this way is often misunderstood. It shows up quietly and politely, like, "Hello, I'm here because someone loved you. Please don't send me straight to the mall."

The fastest way to make inheritance money disappear is to treat it as "extra" or "found" money; something to be spent rather than stewarded. History is full of cautionary tales: lottery winners, sudden heirs, windfalls that vanish within a few years. It's so common that the phrase "shirtsleeves to shirtsleeves in three generations" exists for a reason. But this report is designed to interrupt that story.

When you regulate this money as energy, as we discussed in earlier chapters, and consciously manage its outflows, something remarkable happens. Instead of a one-time event, it becomes a continuing stream. Cash flow that can support you for the rest of your life... and possibly your children, grandchildren, or causes you care deeply about. In Flow-Grow terms, inheritance isn't a finish line. It's a hand-off. And when treated with intention, it can keep running, long after the initial moment of loss has passed.

?_____

9.9

Divorce Alimony

If you receive alimony, or child support, capture the total here. Terms vary widely: amounts, time limits, conditions, and the payer's actual ability to pay. This is one of those sources where strategic planning is essential. Know your timeline. Know your alternatives. Know what your life looks like after this flow ends. This may be the time to acquire knowledge and skills that will prove valuable if this flow changes."

?_____

9.10

Credit

Ah yes, credit, the financial frenemy. We already discussed this under Negative Assets, so you know the heart of it: Using debt shrinks your value over time, even though 41% of American households earning $50K–$100K use credit cards for basic needs. https://civicscience.com/more-than-40-of-american-households-rely-on-credit-cards-to-pay-the-bills-leading-to-a-vicious-debt-cycle/ (Yes, that number is real. No, you are not alone.)

For the Flow-Grow report, we're not judging. We're measuring. If you paid your balance to zero every month? Great, enter nothing. But if you carried a balance all year, paid interest, and ended the year still owing money, then you did rely on credit as an energy source. To calculate this:

- Add your monthly balances
- Divide by twelve
- Enter that number

This gives you a clear picture of how much "energy" came from borrowing. Awareness doesn't punish you. It just gives you the steering wheel back.

?____

9.11

Capital Gains

Capital Gains, the category that sometimes arrives quietly with a whisper, and other times bursts through the door like it's carrying a television-sized lottery check. This can be the blockbuster income item of your year.

Some years, capital gains are small. Maybe you or your broker sold a handful of stocks because the market was having one of its mood swings and it seemed wise to take a little profit. Other years? A house sells. A rental property sells. A business sells. Or your share of a family business is bought out. Suddenly the number on the page looks less like an income line and more like a plot twist.

The beauty of capital gains is that they are taxed differently from ordinary income. This is the government's way of saying, "Thank you for contributing to capitalism. Please enjoy this discounted tax rate."

If you sell your primary residence, and you've lived there long enough, you may qualify for a tax-free chunk of that gain. An amount so generous it almost feels suspicious, as though the IRS forgot to proofread. Dan and I have moved ten times in the last 30 years. Most every time, we were able to improve our net worth. This has been our most reliable source of growth.

If you sell an income property, things get more complex. There are depreciation recaptures, 1031 exchanges, long-term vs. short-term rates, holding periods, and enough tax strategies to make your accountant visibly light up.

Here's the important contemplative-financial point: This income source can be profoundly impactful, but it comes with rules. The IRS will not simply take your word for it. You must conform to timelines, criteria, and structures, not unlike following recipe steps if you want the soufflé to rise instead of collapse into a sad pancake.

So track your capital gains carefully. Record them clearly. And get good advice when the numbers get big enough to make your eyes widen. Because a well-managed capital gain is not just money, it's a surge of energy that can propel your entire Flow-Grow™ ecosystem forward.

?_____

9.12

Miscellaneous (a.k.a. "The Drawer of Mystery")

There is a line for "miscellaneous." Think of this as your financial junk drawer – the place where all the oddball income goes when it refuses to behave and fit into any respectable category. You want the whole revenue picture, so it's worth scooping up these stray coins and curiosities into one total figure.

A good way to check whether you've accurately identified your real income categories is this: miscellaneous should not swell beyond 20% of the whole. If it does, that's the universe politely whispering, "Friend, you've missed something important."

On the flip side, if you've listed something above this line that delivers only pennies and pocket lint, don't give it the red-carpet treatment – slide it down into miscellaneous where it can hang out with its natural tribe.

Like life, money loves clarity. And like a junk drawer, this category should be small enough that you can still close it without using both hands and your foot.

?_____

9.13

Gifts

Ah, gifts – the surprise money that arrives in everything from birthday checks to a fully paid vacation. If someone pays for something on your behalf, that is energy flowing into your life. Record the value of it. This includes:

- Birthday money
- Holiday envelopes

- Tuition someone else covered
- A friend who treated you to a trip
- A relative who paid for a medical procedure
- A forgiven loan (yes, that counts!)

These can even have tax implications, which means your Flow-Grow sheet might someday save you from conversations that start with, "Why is the IRS sending me love letters?" More importantly, as your personal CFO, you must recognize when your life is being subsidized by others. This is not about shame — it's about clarity.

If you live with a relative, estimate what that housing would cost at market rate. Not the "family discount" price. The actual price. Enter it as a gift, and list who is providing it. Why? Because independence is part of adult thriving — Maslow thought so, the animal kingdom confirms it, and Daniel Siegel's concept of "Minding" underscores it.

Some people genuinely cannot yet support themselves due to environmental or social barriers. This is real and deserves compassion. But if you're reading this book, your task is to see your true energy flows so you can begin steering your life toward growth.

And yes, this may be uncomfortable. But mindfulness is not about comfort — it's about awareness. Think of Vipassana meditation: you scan the body, not to fix anything, but to observe. And magically, once you become aware you're slouching, you sit up straighter — not because you barked at yourself, but because awareness made the next healthier action obvious.

Your financial energy responds the same way.

?_____

CHAPTER 10

FLOW-GROW ENERGY USES

10.1

Uses or Allocations of Energy

Let's take a step back from the spreadsheet rows for a moment and zoom out to the balcony view of your life. I want you to imagine yourself, truly, as the Chief Executive Officer of You, Inc. Your mission is not mere survival. Your mission is to thrive with strategy, sass, and sovereignty.

This book is not another financial self-help manual·trying to tell you which magic stock or investment trend is guaranteed to make you rich. That's adorable, but we've all lived long enough to know that markets are basically moody teenagers: unpredictable, dramatic, and absolutely uninterested in following generic rules. What is predictable? Your own patterns of energy. And that's where we start.

This right side of your Flow–Grow Report shows how you're allocating your energy; your life force, your attention, your bandwidth. And knowing this about yourself is essential for what scientists (and Daniel Siegel) call regulation. It's also essential for what I call staying sane while building wealth. This book gives you a framework, not to tell yourself stories, excuses, or little white lies ("I only doom-scrolled for five minutes!"). No. We are grounding ourselves in actuals, not mythology.

You'll notice I've included some example rows for illustration. These include: Housing, food, transportation, etc. Please insert and delete them without remorse and enter your real categories. Rearrange them from largest to smallest. Let the truth appear on the page, softly, gently, even playfully, but truthfully. Because here's the thing:

This process isn't about meeting someone else's standard. It's about observing who you are. No judgment. No shame. Just data. Consider this your personal baseline. The starting line, not the finish line. It's infinitely more powerful than a budget, because budgets are often fiction; wishful thinking in Excel form. But your Flow-Grow Report? That's an x-ray.

Women will vary wildly in what their numbers look like. A 28-year-old and a 78-year-old might have absolutely nothing in common on paper, and yet, emotionally, feel exactly the same: like they're starting from scratch. Some of us begin with nothing, or less than nothing. Some of us begin with resources we didn't even realize were resources. It doesn't matter.

If you haven't heard of it, there is a strategy called "Pay Yourself First," which is a strategic way to think of your cash outflow. That you, in essence, decide to direct at least 10% of your cash allocation to a performing savings vehicle ***before*** any other allocation. What this means is that you will make choices for housing, food, transportation based on the money that remains. You might think of it as a "tithe." But that's only one strategy.

As you review your actual cash expenditures against your cash inflow, you may be dismayed that you can't make ends meet. ***This is a good thing.*** It means you are seeing things "as they are," a necessary step in mindfulness practice. Today can be Day One. And yes, it may yield surprises. Surprises wake us up. They nudge us toward mindfulness about "minding," that ability to regulate your energy and information with clarity instead of chaos.

That clarity will provide the momentum for change. If you feel you can't change, then it may be time to seek help. You may be "stuck" as Charlotte Kasl eloquently describes in her book ***If The Buddha Got Stuck.*** She offers some helpful strategies to get unstuck.

But, have compassion for yourself, remember, you may not have the skill and practice at self-regulation yet. You may need professional help in making choices about housing, food, child care, or expenses that seem overwhelming. Remember, I initially felt that I wanted to keep my beautiful house after my divorce. It was only after I got unstuck about that, I was able to sell the house and experience a sense of relief and freedom. But almost more importantly, it gave me the spark of faith in my own ability to shift when it was necessary. It didn't feel like going backwards, it felt like growing up. And in the next section I'll offer a way to re-frame your thinking about set-backs, obstacles, and life challenges.

?_____

10.2

Housing

Housing deserves special attention because it will likely be the largest expenditure decision of your life. Many of us approach housing decisions based on what we saw growing up in our own families. That's natural. But before you simply repeat those patterns, consider this: You are learning to think about money as the allocation of energy.

During your 20s, 30s, and even into your 40s, you will typically have your highest levels of personal energy available to invest in your future. These are the decades when you can work hard, build skills, experiment, and pursue growth. One wise strategy during these years is to make efficient housing choices, in other words, choices that require the least amount of your energy.

It is easy to become seduced by the idea of larger or grander housing. Sometimes we want homes that resemble what our parents had, or what we imagine success should look like. You will hear a great deal of advice about what you "can afford." A common guideline suggests spending 20–30% of your income on housing. Some enthusiastic brokers may even stretch that to 35–40%.

But let's pause for a moment. If you think of housing primarily as a structure that protects you from the elements and provides safety, health, and well-being, rather than as performative space, generous guest quarters, or a form of bragging rights, you may discover that smaller is often wiser, especially in the early years. At least until you begin developing performing assets.

I remember the first house I bought with my first husband. It was a modest little place; about 700 square feet, one bedroom and one bathroom. There was no garage, not even a carport. And the hill was so steep that we had to check the handbrake carefully and turn the tires into the curb. But there was one thing that mattered: Location.

The house sat on West Highland Drive on Queen Anne Hill in Seattle. While the property itself was humble, the neighborhood was one of the best in the city. Over time, we slowly improved the house so that it began to match the quality of the neighborhood. In the language of this book, you might say we were investing in Physical Mind Money. Allocations like that can appreciate for you.

In fact, choosing a modest home in a strong neighborhood, and improving it gradually, has been one of the most successful strategies I've followed over the past thirty years. Sometimes the most powerful financial move is not buying more house, but buying better context.

?_____

10.3

Credit Card Interest

This is a category worth paying attention to, and studying with clear eyes. Credit card interest is one of the least consumer-friendly corners of the financial world. Some rates exceed 25%, which means that over time you may end up paying more than double the original purchase price. That's not a small detail.

Still, credit cards themselves are not inherently evil. They are tools. Used thoughtfully, they can be convenient and even useful. Some cards offer introductory periods with 0% interest, for example, which can make sense if you are absolutely confident you can pay off the balance within the specified time frame. (You can see examples of these offers here: https://www.forbes.com/advisor/credit-cards/best-0-apr-credit-cards/.) The key word here is confident.

If you begin to feel overwhelmed or unsure about repayment, that is a signal worth respecting. In that case, it may be wise to consult a reputable debt advisor and get clear guidance before the interest meter keeps running.

As a general rule, here is the system that works for me: I pay off the entire balance every month. In that way, the card functions more like an expense tracker than a borrowing device. I pay no interest at all. In exchange for a modest annual fee, we earn travel miles that we occasionally use for trips. Other cards offer cash-back rewards, which can serve a similar purpose.

But keep your net worth in mind. Any outstanding credit balance reduces it. The arithmetic is simple. One helpful way to frame the decision is to pause and ask yourself:

"Would I still want to buy this item, or have this experience, if I had to pay for it directly from my own savings?"

That single question can save you a surprising amount of money—and stress.

?____

10.4

Gifts, Grants, and Donations

Some readers may reach a point where they have the resources to allocate energy toward gifts, grants, or charitable donations. In the language of this book, these often fall into the category of Community Mind Money; investments in the well-being of others. This can be deeply meaningful. Giving is one of the ways wealth becomes relational rather than purely personal.

But it is worth pausing for a moment of honest reflection. If you are currently paying interest on credit cards or loans, you might ask yourself a simple question: Is this generosity coming from growth, or from the desire for approval? There is no judgment here, only awareness. Sometimes the most responsible act of generosity is first strengthening your own financial footing. When your foundation is stable, your giving becomes both freer and more sustainable.

At the same time, these choices carry tax implications. As financial systems become increasingly transparent through digital tracking, it is wise to understand the rules before making significant commitments. When in doubt, consult a qualified professional. A thoughtful conversation with a tax advisor can help ensure that your generosity aligns with both your intentions and the practical realities of the financial system.

Giving is most satisfying when it is both heartfelt and well-informed.

?____

10.5

A Note on Growth and Creativity (Your Secret Weapons)

You'll see I added two specific rows to the energy-allocation side: Growth and Creativity. These are the life-affirming muscles I will evangelize about until your eyes roll back in your head, but lovingly. If there is one recommendation I will make, it is this: Track how much money (energy) you spend on your personal growth. Then also log it as a Mind Money asset. It's not indulgence; it's capital.

Creativity, meanwhile, is your superpower. Not the "paint watercolors while wearing linen pants" creativity, though good for you if that's your style. I mean the kind of creativity that lets you take the existing threads of your life and weave them into a totally new pattern. Creativity gets you out of credit-card disasters, into better jobs, and through unexpected windfalls without making terrible decisions. It is a muscle, and like any muscle, it improves with training and support. I'll share one story about spending money to gain expertise.

?_____

10.6

A Story About Creativity That Re-ignited My Career

There was a chapter of my life when I stepped out of the workforce for several years to try (every version of) fertility treatments. At the end of that journey, when it was clear that parenthood wasn't meant to be, I wanted to work again, but I'd lost confidence. I didn't know how to explain a three-year gap. I felt like I'd been swallowed by a hole.

Then I saw an ad for Career Improvement Group in Seattle, run by a man named Dennis Buckmaster. It was essentially a master's degree in career reinvention. Six months, $3,500—a big leap. But I knew: This became my Growth line item. It paid off.

One of the hardest lessons was learning how to repurpose my skills creatively, across industries I didn't even know I was qualified for. Suddenly I was interviewing at:

- an Art College
- Berlitz Language School
- city utility offices
- and ultimately, an aircraft switch company

It was only after I creatively reframed my shipyard purchasing experience that the aircraft company saw me clearly. And offered me a salary far higher than I'd imagined. Which leads me to a simple philosophy: Don't be a gamer. Be a game changer.

?_____

10.7

The Bottom Line

Any creative endeavor: art, music, design, improv, woodworking, pottery, dance, writing, strengthens your ability to reimagine your life. It's not a luxury. It's a tool of liberation. And it is absolutely worth allocating energy (and money) toward. Pay someone to help you learn it. Then log it as Knowledge. That way it adds another asset to your self worth. Because creativity doesn't just help you solve problems. It helps you become someone who creates her own possibilities. I'll talk more about this in Section 11.5 "Creativity Cures Crisis."

?_____

CHAPTER 11

SIX BELIEFS FOR STRESS RELIEF

I used to start all my wholistic wealth presentations with the Six Beliefs because, frankly, women deserve relief before they deserve more information. Studies show that women are excellent at managing the day-to-day money, the grocery trips, the bill paying, the juggling act that would put any Wall Street trader to shame. But when it comes to asset management, our stress levels spike like a seismograph during an earthquake.

So opening with stress reduction felt sensible. But at the end of each class, I would ask my students, "How can I do this better?" One brilliant woman said, "Maybe reverse the order. Younger women might want to get straight to the numbers before talking about beliefs." Fair point. Gen Z wants their data before their dharma.

And for this book, I realized she was right: Beliefs belong at the end, after you've actually counted. After you know your numbers, that's when you're ready for the deeper framework, the wind beneath your wings. That's when you need to understand the currents, the waves, the stabilizers. You're not just driving your financial car anymore, you're learning to fly it. The beliefs that follow are meant to help you internalize a profound truth:

As you grow from childhood to adulthood, you have the power to adopt new beliefs that actually serve your navigation. You are no longer navigating by what Mommy and Daddy believed. You are navigating by the stars. And those stars form guiding constellations, which are formed by both ancient patterns and your own choices. These suggested beliefs come from a lifetime of studying business, personal growth, and contemplative philosophy, They are tested, not just in theory, but in the lived messiness of a real life. Mine, to be exact.

?____

11.1

A Very Old Guide for a Very Modern Woman: Mettá Sutta

An ancient guide turns out to be surprisingly useful in everyday life. Older than any religious system still standing, older than any contemporary self-help model, originally written in Sanskrit. I don't read Sanskrit, but I can tell you exactly how I first became acquainted with it.

I was stumbling my way through an MFA at Naropa University, at the tender age of sixty. Picture me trying to write 10,000 words per semester in both creative and critical essays. Like learning to swim in Niagara Falls while someone hands you a pencil and says, "Write something insightful on your way down."

One day, a teacher named Robert Spellman walked by and said to a group of undergraduates, "My class on Mettá Sutta starts in room 201." I didn't know what it was, but my curiosity perked up. I asked if I could attend. Spellman said yes with the kind of graciousness that makes you feel like an honored guest instead of someone who wandered into the wrong century.

The material was simple enough, but the atmosphere, Spellman's presence, made it feel powerful. The Mettá Sutta is often practiced as a mantra:

"May I feel safe.

May I feel healthy.

May I feel joyful.

May I feel free."

He said you could recite it for yourself, and you could also send that same "energy" (his words) to another person or even to all beings: "May all feel safe, healthy, joyful, and free." Here's what struck me: he didn't say ***be*** safe. He said *feel* safe. The mantra isn't about perfection in your outer circumstances. It's about your internal sensations, your embodied reality. It's a meditative check-in, a quiet inner inventory.

And that's when a lightbulb went on: This mantra could be a measuring tool. Another way to "count" your life. An emotional dashboard. So in my classes, I suggest to ask yourself:

Do I feel safe?

Do I feel healthy?

Do I feel joyful?

Do I feel free?

Rate each one from one to ten. Or simply say yes or no. Either way, you now have another Mind Money metric. One that tells you whether your choices are moving you toward growth or away from it. If you answer "no," that's your signal: something needs to shift.

It pairs beautifully with Maslow's hierarchy of needs, which, in a way, is simply another ancient form of energetic accounting.

Do I Feel Safe?

This is foundational. Do you feel safe with your partner? Safe with family? Safe in your home? In your neighborhood? At your workplace? Your chosen institutions? In your town or country? If safety is compromised, everything else becomes harder. Safety is the first pillar of wholistic wealth.

Do I Feel Healthy?

This requires body-awareness, the ability to listen to the internal signals you've been expertly trained to ignore. We evolved to move, forage, hunt, gather, cultivate. Now we tap, click, and DoorDash. Our food systems have shifted from personal labor to industrial agribusiness, and our bodies are often the ones sounding the alarm.

Your body grades you daily. The question is: are you listening? This is one of the most essential examples of learning to assess your own energy and information. Sometimes that information needs to be based on tests. For example, we've recently started working with a Functional Health practitioner. The tests she ordered disclosed several imbalances that deserve attention. Not in the emergency medical sense, but more like, lets do some things to help your cells and organs improve their function to get you back in balance. Every dollar we spend on this treatment is captured in Physical Mind Money. And this year, our Flow-Grow report will reflect that energy investment.

Do I Feel Joyful?

Somewhere along the way, joy became complicated. But the ancient ones were onto something simple: joy comes from presence. From being aligned inside and out. From being in nature, or in creativity, or in connection. Joy is not a purchase. Joy is a resonance.

When we moved to St. George, Utah, three years ago, we were stunned by the beauty of the intensely stained sandstone rock formations and the way the sun's progress created a procession throughout the day. Every sense was treated to a unique experience both subtle and deep. We poured our joy into a book project called *Collabitation*, which you can see at the website studiodecouvrir.com. We spend time each day renewing that sense of joy.

Some of the women I talk to sometimes experience a kind of numbness, sadness, or depression. It happens to ***every single one*** of us at some point. But I've found that one potent antidote is to allow our senses to rest on the smallest details of nature: the ripples in water, the movement of a small bird, the way a branch moves in the breeze, the sounds of a forest, or the scent of a crushed blade of grass. Sometimes I imagine that the most valuable question between friends is to ask "what has brought you joy today?"

Do I Feel Free?

This one is deceptively profound. Freedom is rare in the world, and fragile. It requires vigilance. It requires choice. It requires responsibility.

My father, a lifelong student of philosophy, once asked me, "Would you rather be safe or free?" The question still echoes through my life. And perhaps I'm idealistic, but I believe we should insist on both.

In Conclusion

I offer you the belief that this ancient mantra, the Mettá Sutta, can serve as your personal emotional yardstick. A measuring device that clarifies your feelings, illuminates your choices, and supports your wholistic wealth journey. Because at the end of the day, how you feel is both data and destiny. And you have the power to make choices every day to improve those measures.

?_____

11.2

Nothing is Wrong (With You): A Curative Faith

About halfway through my coach training for mindfulness coaching, I woke up one morning with the distinct sense that something heavy had slipped off my body in the night, like an emotional sandbag had simply decided it was bored with me and rolled away. In today's terms, it was Ozempic for the mind: a sudden shedding of something bloated and unhealthy that I hadn't even realized I was carrying. What disappeared was that constant background buzzing that whispered, "Something is wrong." And if I'm honest, the whisper usually finished the sentence with: "and that something is you."

That hum had been with me for so long I assumed it was factory-installed. So I coped the way so many accomplished women cope: by managing every detail, by being prepared enough for three lifetimes, by studying harder than necessary, by being gracious when I wanted to roll my eyes, by smiling through the exhaustion. All that energy spent trying to outrun an invisible flaw.

And then, one day... it was gone.

It felt like stepping over a threshold and finding myself in a different landscape entirely, as if I had wandered (accidentally!) into a small, private Garden of Eden. A world washed clean. A world where breath itself felt new.

It reminded me, unexpectedly, of Rodin's sculpture "Je Suis Belle," the figure who seems to discover her own form in mid-motion, as though catching sight of herself for the very first time and recognizing, with a shock of truth: I am beautiful. Not by comparison, not by permission, simply because the veil has lifted and she can finally see what was always there.

And, if you take this book seriously, you won't need a man to do the sculpting. Some men even adopt a kind of "Pygmalian" strategy so that they can promise to help create a more fully developed woman. It's better to avoid that trap, the kind of predatory promises that work on the young and vulnerable. Instead, you will have the tools from this book to manifest who you are as you will have information to create yourself.

But that was the feeling: a startling, almost innocent recognition of my own enoughness.

There are many ways to reach this doorway. I won't pretend there's a shortcut. No spiritual express lane where enlightenment merges seamlessly into daily life. But I will say this: arriving at the belief that nothing is wrong with you is transformational. You are the perfect product of your formative conditions. It is the internal equivalent of being handed back the keys to your own life.

Dan Siegel's work helped me understand why that belief is so life-changing. He writes about two foundational forces: attachment style and personal narrative. Attachment is shaped by the parenting we received, how we learned to read the world's signals about safety, love, and belonging. Narrative is the story we eventually learn to tell ourselves about all of that.

Most parents never got the instruction manual. They relied on instinct, memory, neighbors, and the occasional expert. My mother once mentioned Dr. Spock, whose passion for "fresh air" meant we spent half our childhood in Washington Square Park, no matter the season. Parents do their best with the tools they have.

But Siegel's real contribution is integrating modern neuroscience with mindfulness. He reframes childhood development not as a list of rules, but as a dynamic system of wiring and rewiring. A child's brain grows through connection, conversation, and the careful naming of feelings. And, this is the liberating part, the adult brain can, too.

Our "coping strategies" are not character defects. They're adaptive responses that made sense then, even if they limit us now. We are the perfect products of our environments. In my case, the emotional climate of my childhood trained me to take responsibility. I believed that if I were competent enough, good enough, calm enough, helpful enough, everything would be okay. That strategy worked for a long time. Until it didn't.

By midlife, the old coping patterns trapped me. The buzzing grew louder. The "wrongness" script got heavier. I hit a crisis point. But I was extraordinarily fortunate: my pivot came at 40, and the decade that followed, yes, a full decade, was a slow walk toward a new way of being. Only now, on the far side of that threshold, can I articulate what I've learned in a way that feels whole enough to share.

So here is the belief that changed everything for me: If you can release the idea that something is wrong with you, and instead meet life's uncertainty with faith in your ability to improvise, you will be free. Every moment is an opportunity to choose differently. It's not reckless faith, not magical thinking. It's a grounded, resilient, quietly powerful faith that fills you up. The kind that grows from knowing yourself, and allowing the unknown around you to unfold.

In other words, faith is sturdier than desire. Desire clings to outcomes. Faith roots you in your own capacity. And when you count on yourself from that place, the whole world begins to open, like Rodin's figure turning toward her own form and realizing, perhaps for the first time: Je suis belle.

I am whole. I am enough. And nothing is wrong with me *that can't be improved by a different choice from this moment on..*

?_____

11.3

Energy and Information

We touched on this earlier, but it deserves a spotlight here at the end of the journey, because it is a belief that will serve you for the rest of your life: Minding is the regulation of energy and information.

Dan Siegel says this often, and once it sinks in, you begin to see it everywhere. It's as practical as driving a car: you take in information from the road, speed limit signs, brake lights, weather, the occasional rogue tumbleweed, and you regulate your energy output through pedals, steering, and attention to get where you want to go.

Life works the same way. Only now you are the car, the driver, *and* the GPS. To move through life's highways, its straightaways, traffic jams, surprise detours, and breathtaking overlooks, you must learn to regulate your own energy in response to real information. Not fantasies. Not fears. Not inherited scripts about what you "should" do. But actual data.

And here's the liberating part: When you get good at noticing Information and choosing how to allocate your Energy, you will outperform most people in nearly every arena of life. Why? Because most people are exhausted reactors, not conscious regulators. They burn fuel on the wrong things, the wrong people, the wrong interpretations, the wrong stories. Meanwhile, you, armed with awareness, learn to spend energy where it counts and conserve it where it doesn't.

This belief becomes especially powerful in organizational life. If you've ever wondered what founders, CEOs, or visionary leaders actually do, here's the secret: They regulate the energy and information of their entire corporate system. They're scanning the horizon. Reading patterns. Tracking feedback loops. Adjusting flow.

And they desperately need people within the organization who can do this too. Employees who serve as intelligent sensors and strategic allies rather than passive instruments.

If you speak this language, if you can identify where information is missing or where energy is being wasted, you instantly become indispensable. Particularly in today's technology-driven, fast-moving environments, where every startup begins as a swirling chaos of good ideas and insufficient structure. Someone has to stabilize the system. Someone has to connect the feedback loops. Someone has to say, "Let's make sure the left hand knows what the right hand is building."

This is the superpower: Women who learn to regulate energy and information become the steady heartbeats inside organizations.

Let me give you a real example. At one point in my career, I did what I lovingly called a "walk-about," the corporate version of wandering the village to see how everyone's doing. I wandered into the customer-pricing division, where estimators worked like quiet geniuses. Truly, they were the heartbeat of the company. They took a customer's dream, turned it into parts and design, calculated materials, labor, overhead, general and administrative costs, sprinkled on a necessary profit margin, and handed back a number that kept the whole operation afloat.

But as I listened to them, something felt off. So I asked one simple question: "Do you have a way to compare your estimated price with the actual cost of building and delivering the project?"They looked at me and said, "No." Not sheepishly, just matter-of-factly. It had never occurred to them. I smiled and said, "You might want to think about that."That's it. No lecture. No spreadsheet. No six-sigma analysis. Just a gentle nudge in the direction of information.

Within a year, that department had created exactly that report.

And instantly, they became even smarter. That's the power of closing a feedback loop. That's the power of noticing missing information. That's the power of minding.

When you understand energy and information, really understand it, you begin to organize your own life the way great leaders organize companies: Clear channels. Aligned effort. Thoughtful expenditure. Minimal waste. Maximum clarity. And the beautiful part? This belief doesn't make life easier, it makes you more skillful. It gives you back the steering wheel. It hands you the keys to your mind. It prepares you for turbulence and tailwinds alike.

Energy and information: a simple idea, a lifelong strategy, and one of the most profound tools for women learning to count on themselves.

11.4

Emotions and Money Are Energy

Why is this a useful belief? Because when you adopt the earlier idea that minding is the regulation of energy and information, you suddenly see emotions and money in a new light. They're not just "data." They are energy sources, often the loudest, flashiest, most persuasive motivators in human life. And the sooner you learn to regulate them, the smoother the navigation gets. It's like moving from driving a grocery-getter to handling a glider: less jerky reaction, more intentional flight.

Let's consider emotions through the lens of evolution. Every organism evolves the ability to sense its environment because the ones who didn't, well, didn't make it. But because staying hyper-vigilant would burn too much fuel, evolution gifted us an efficiency system. psychologist Daniel Kahneman described this beautifully as System 1 (fast, automatic) versus System 2 (slow, deliberate).

Nature, being a savvy energy manager, made sure that we "fire up" the big emotions only when survival or opportunity is at stake.

Daniel Siegel's work also aligns with this deeply. In ***The Whole Brain Child,*** he describes the emotional centers as the "downstairs brain" — the older, primal structures that rev up instantly to keep us alive. These "downstairs" systems activate hormones that sharpen our senses, boost our strength, and give us the energy burst we need to fight, flee, freeze, or embrace. Emotions, in other words, are natural energy amplifiers.

A moment from the documentary ***InnSæi*** (The Sea Within) has stayed with me for years. A boy explains that he used to be terrified of his father's anger, until he learned that this "big scary emotion" came from a brain structure designed to protect us from danger. Once he understood that the emotion wasn't about him, something softened. He stopped personalizing it. I remember thinking, "Where was this class when I was eight?"

Love, on the other hand, is also an energy amplifier. It comes from similar ancient circuitry: bonding, procreating, protecting the tribe. When we learn where these feelings originate, we stop expecting them to behave like logical accountants. Greed, envy, disgust — they all trigger systems designed to mobilize our bodies toward action. Once you see this, you can regulate your emotions more skillfully. You become the person who knows how to drive a race car on the track, not while trying to merge onto Main Street at rush hour.

And what about money? If energy is the potential for action, then money is the vehicle that carries that potential. It's the symbolic fuel that lets us access things and experiences we want. That makes money emotionally charged. Sometimes too charged. When emotions and money sit too close together, wires can cross. People sometimes mistake money for love. Sometimes it's a substitute; sometimes it's an expression. But it's never the same as presence, attention, or safety. Skill grows when you learn to tell the difference.

Children raised with scarcity often develop either rigid or chaotic coping strategies, as Siegel describes. Those strategy-patterns follow us into adulthood unless we bring them into awareness. That is why doing your Grow-Flow Report each year is so important: it reveals whether your emotional patterns around money are evolving, stabilizing, or asking for some mindful renovation.

The point isn't to eliminate emotion. It's to recognize its energetic impact. When you can regulate both emotions and money, two of the most powerful forces in your daily life, you're no longer being swept along by the current. You're learning how to steer.

?_____

11.5

Creativity Cures Crises

We talked earlier in the Flow–Grow section about building your creative muscles. Think of creativity as the emotional equivalent of Pilates: at first you're not sure what's happening, then suddenly you can lift things you never thought possible; like your mood, your marriage, or your sense of hope after receiving a surprise letter from the IRS.

Years ago, when I was developing my singer-songwriter career, I desperately wanted better stage presence. There's a saying that nothing clears a room faster than a sincere folksinger strumming intensely about feelings. I say this with love because, at the time – that was me. People weren't exactly running for the exits, but there was a kind of slow, quiet migration toward the bathrooms.

So I tried to learn how to be funny. First stop: a class with Danny

Simon, the funny brother of playwright Neil Simon. Turns out humor is not hereditary by proximity. Lovely man. Wrong student. Nothing "took."

Second stop: Kim Schultz, trained with Second City in Chicago. This worked. Kim's approach to improvisation rested on two glorious pillars:

- Authenticity: which means showing up as yourself, not the fictional character you wish you were on LinkedIn.
- Say yes, not in a reckless "Sure, I'll adopt six ferrets" way, but in a creative "Let's see where this goes" way.

This combination was revolutionary. Suddenly my performances loosened up. I found myself having actual fun on stage. I even wrote a playful relationship song inspired by my husband. He will absolutely pretend he's mortified that I'm mentioning it here, but rest assured: he secretly enjoys being the muse.

You don't have to buy me flowers, jewels, or sweets

I don't need fancy dinners or island retreats

If we lose our way, to the garden we knew

Well, here's a path for you

Like an artist paints a picture and chooses a hue

Draws a line suggesting a view

Let me offer a new way, then you can improvise

Just tell me beautiful lies

Ch: *Tell me you drink the scent of me in*

Tell me your lips need the taste of my skin

Tell me you see paradise in my eyes,

Just tell me beautiful lies... Beautiful lies

Say it feels like new, not like years
Tell me that movie moved you to tears
Say you'd rather be together, than out with the guys
Just tell me beautiful lies
Ch:
Bridge: Sometimes a story is like a master key
That opens the door – to me...
Say the day flew just thinking of me
And traffic was clear to our door
Say I'm still the one, that makes your sun rise
Just tell me beautiful lies, Beautiful Lies...
Ch:

Kim also revealed one of life's great truths: poignancy and comedy are step-sisters. They share a bunk bed and steal each other's sweaters. If you tilt almost any sad moment by ten degrees, it becomes funny. And if you tilt something funny by ten degrees, suddenly you're crying in the grocery store. Improvisation teaches you how to surf that emotional tilt without wiping out.

Creativity helped me recover from my divorce too. It gave me permission to say "yes" to things that felt improbable, unreasonable, or simply new. It also reframed the meaning of "no." In negotiation training I learned that "no" is just a first offer, which is a very empowering thought when you're rebuilding your life —or asking someone out for coffee.

If you've watched ***A Discovery of Witches***, you might remember the heroine seeing glowing threads in the air and weaving them into magic. That is exactly what creativity feels like, minus the helpful CGI. You start noticing tiny threads everywhere: odd ideas, unexpected coincidences, sudden insights, the cashier who says something weirdly profound while bagging your groceries. Those threads are invitations. When you weave them together, you create new possibilities.

Creativity doesn't just help you through a crisis. It hands you a loom and says, "Here, make something better than what you started with."

?_____

11.6

Growth As a Life Purpose

This belief didn't arrive gently. It didn't float in on a breeze or descend on a lotus petal. No, it came up behind me in midlife and whacked me on the back of the head like a spiritual two-by-four. The message?

> **Growth, not achievement, not fame, not perfection, is the actual purpose of a human life.**

To be clear, I was never a fan of "life purpose" talk. It always sounded like a marketing campaign for people who already knew what they wanted to be when they grew up: astronauts, firemen, conductors, future Nobel laureates. Meanwhile I was over here thinking, "I just want a library pass and a quiet corner."

In high school, a producer even offered me a spot as the lead singer in a band he was developing. For about ten minutes, I felt very Janis Ian, who had skyrocketed to fame right out of our shared

Music & Art High School. But then he said I'd have to skip college. And something in me, probably the same inner compass that keeps me from believing limited-time offers, said, "Nope. Not happening." Fame looked a little too seductive and not nearly balanced enough.

Fast forward to my sixth decade, when I was in MFA classes at Naropa, deep in the study of women who had become spiritual leaders, healing forces, cultural anchors. And then I met Hildegard von Bingen — on the page, not in a vision, though frankly with Hildegard you never know.

She lived from 1098 to 1179 in the German town of Disibodenberg, and she was what we'd call today a genius rock star: visionary, composer, philosopher, naturalist, abbess, healer, and occasional correspondent to powerful men who probably didn't know what hit them. She'd spent years sequestered in a monastery with her cousin and every book they could get their hands on. From this cloistered, book-soaked childhood came a woman whose ideas have lasted nearly a thousand years. Rather than thinking of her as an "icon," I see her as an intelligent woman philosopher, who used the language of her time in order to thrive.

In her massive Codex, her scholarly collection of writings, she describes a worldview in which the sun represents original energy, and every living thing grows by responding to that energy. Trees, herbs, flowers, and yes, even crystals. (Hildegard might have done very well on Instagram.) Her point was simple and revolutionary:

If everything in nature *grows* toward its source of energy, why should humans be any different?

She even coined a word "Viriditas," which is translated as "Greening," in other words, growth, like a new bud. (Have you ever walked through a forest in early spring and noticed the neon green of such growth?) Faith, she suggested, is trusting that growth is our purpose. Doubt, in that worldview, is simply forgetting this "immutable" relationship of growth towards light.

When I internalized this, something shifted. Suddenly all my past mistakes, every wrong turn, every questionable relationship choice, every financial face-plant, became growth rings instead of indictments. I could finally offer myself the self-compassion required to move forward instead of freeze in shame or regret. And the more compassion I offered myself, the more I could offer others. Maybe they weren't malicious or shallow or unwise; maybe they were simply stuck. Disconnected from the perennial source of growth.

Charlotte Kasl's wonderful book ***If the Buddha Got Stuck*** made this even clearer: stuckness is not a character flaw; it's a temporary condition curable by awareness, curiosity, and movement. Despite best wishes of friends and family, no one can unstick us but ourselves.

Since adopting this belief, I've found it much easier to forgive myself, apologize when needed, and stop treating my past like a crime scene. Mistakes became educational instead of humiliating. Some even became funny. (In hindsight, with snacks.)

There are plenty of opportunities in life to blow it, with money, with relationships, with judgment calls that make you wince years later. But when growth is your life purpose, mistakes stop being disasters. They become compost. And compost, as Hildegard would remind us, is just fuel for the next round of blooming.

?_____

EPILOGUE: COUNTING ON YOURSELF—YOUR WORTH AND REBIRTH

As you come to the end of this book, you may notice something subtle but unmistakable: you've been doing a kind of quiet excavation. You've gathered numbers, tracked assets, evaluated patterns, explored emotions, and tugged gently at the threads connecting energy, information, and your lived experience. You've gathered the data of your life, and then, just as importantly, you've interpreted that data with compassion.

That is the heart of the Financial Selfie. Not the totals. Not the formulas. The self part.

You've also discovered that wealth is not just about bank balances. It's about Mind Money, the currencies of gratitude, experience, mentorship, physical vitality, creativity, insight, community, and knowledge. These are the assets that don't fluctuate with market swings and don't evaporate when interest rates rise. They increase with use, attention, and presence.

And perhaps you've also seen that Flow–Grow is not a magical philosophy but a practical rhythm. An honest assessment of where your energy is flowing and where you'd like it to grow. A reminder that life is not static and you don't have to be either. Even a small shift in direction, financial, emotional, or energetic, counts as movement.

Finally, the Six Beliefs offered you a framework that, if nothing else, reminds you that you're human. You have a brain designed in layers. You have emotions that act like energetic weather patterns. You have money stories that didn't start with you. You have creativity waiting to be invited to the conversation. And you have a built-in capacity for growth, even when circumstances temporarily convince you otherwise.

If you've reached this point in the book, you've already demonstrated one of the most important beliefs: you're willing to learn. Which means you're willing to grow. Which means, by Hildegard's standards, you're right on purpose.

There may be future mistakes; financial, emotional, relational, and occasionally culinary. (I can only hope yours turn out better than the time I thought a dehydrator could rescue an overzealous batch of broccoli sprouts.) But mistakes lose their sting when you recognize them as tuition. And tuition, as we know, always pays for something.

If there is a final encouragement I want to offer, it is this: Be generous with your future self. She's the one who will benefit from the clarity of your numbers, the steadiness of your habits, the lightness of your humor, and the courage it took to look at every corner of your life with open eyes.

And if you ever doubt your ability to navigate what comes next, remember this: you have already learned about spreadsheets, confronted fears, mapped your mind, reviewed your past, examined your patterns, and kept your sense of humor intact. Frankly, after doing all that, handling your money is going to feel like the easy part.

And one last secret: ***Even if you never do any of this counting, just reading about this way to wholistic wealth will likely change your thinking. You will feel it. You may even find yourself chuckling, "That's worth some Mind Money, honey!"***

So go forward with confidence. Go forward with curiosity. And above all, go forward knowing this: You can count on yourself. And now you know exactly how and why.

?_____

ABOUT THE AUTHOR

Jackie Henrion is a writer, educator, contemplative thinker, and former purchasing executive who spent twenty years negotiating contracts, analyzing data, and discovering, somewhat to her surprise, that corporate procurement is an excellent laboratory for understanding human behavior. After decades of reading the fine print, she now encourages others to read the fine print of their own lives, which turns out to be far more interesting.

Born and raised in New York City's Greenwich Village, she developed a lifelong affection for sharp observation and dry humor, skills honed on subways, in cafés, and in countless moments requiring equal parts patience and curiosity. After thriving in business, she built a creative life as an ASCAP singer-songwriter, performing regularly and studying improvisation with teachers connected to Chicago's famed Second City. These influences infuse her writing with honesty, self-reflection, and just enough comic timing to keep readers breathing during discussions of debt, emotional regulation, and retirement planning.

Jackie spent eight years as host and producer of Songs-Voices-Poems, a weekly radio program on 88.5 KRFY in Sandpoint, Idaho, from 2014 to 2022. Thanks to the miracle of technology, they can still be heard Sundays at 7 pm pst. The show blended poetry, music, and spontaneous storytelling, sharpening her ability to listen deeply, surface meaningful themes, and reveal the humanity behind creative work. She earned her MFA in creative writing from Naropa University, where mindfulness became both a discipline and a survival tool. Her work synthesizes neuroscience, financial literacy, spiritual inquiry, and practical strategy with a clear aim: helping people, especially women, trust themselves enough to build lives of clarity, agency, and grounded wealth.

In developing this book, Jackie used contemporary AI tools for editorial review, while retaining full authorship, voice, and final judgment in every decision. She views such tools not as substitutes for human discernment, but as instruments best used deliberately, in service of clarity, rigor, and creative independence.

She now resides in St. George, Utah, where the sandstone mountains and unbothered roadrunners offer daily reminders that growth often happens in unexpected places.

NOTE FROM JACKIE

I didn't grow up with the word love in my family. I don't know why. And yet I didn't feel deprived because of it. Later, when I began studying mindfulness, I met friends whose version of spirituality could be summed up as, "***The answer is always love.***" I'm thrilled that's worked for them.

But, as you've probably sensed throughout this book, my own understanding of love has been shaped less by such declarations and more by knowing myself; mostly through intellectual curiosity. But I've also carried a quiet awareness that none of us knows how long we'll be here, which makes every moment, every exchange, poignantly precious. So I wanted to take this moment to leave you with something more personal: a song I wrote about the relationship between intellect, heart, body, and spirit. For me, the work of becoming a whole person requires integration and constant re-balance of all these aspects. Perhaps it will resonate with you, my valued reader.

Hello Heart, it's the mind here, it's been a while since we talked

I don't know where the time's gone, but I wondered how you are

You know, I've been busy, running the show

But lately I've been thinking I can't do it alone

So I thought I'd call an old friend for a start

Check in again—hello, Heart

Hello Heart, it's the hands here, been out of touch for an age

We're retired, no demands now, just living page to page

But sometimes we dream about the days of bread and wine

We'd like to raise that glass again, to toast a grand design

So we thought we'd call an old friend for a start

Check in again—hello, Heart

Hello Heart, it's your partner, the one who's been beside you from the start

Sometimes close, sometimes far, like a loom where fate weaves her art

You know, I can't believe we've had this kind of time

And our life's calligraphy started with one line

So I thought I'd draw you out for a start

Check in again—hello, Heart

Well hello—it's the Heart here, I guess I've hidden out for a while

But I must say, it's been an honor to serve you – with a smile

You know, I believe our pulse is music to the stars

Forever reflecting, wherever we are

And I'm glad you took the time to check in before you go

It's the Heart here—hello

Yes, I'm glad you took the time to check in before you go

It's the Heart here—hello

www.ingramcontent.com/pod-product-compliance
Lightning Source LLC
LaVergne TN
LVHW051005080826
845145LV00009B/2462

* 9 7 8 1 7 3 3 1 6 7 2 5 3 *